So schön ist unser Land

Metropole Ruhr

GRILLO-THEATER

So schön ist unser Land

Metropole Ruhr

Von Rainer Kiedrowski (Fotos) und Reinhard Pietsch (Text)

Englisch von Jane Michael

KNESEBECK

Inhalt
Contents

Seite 1: Moers, Halde Rheinpreußen, Grubenlampe von Otto Piene.
Seite 2: Grillo-Stadttheater, Essen, Seiten 3–4: Herdecke, Eisenbahnviadukt.

Page 1: Moers, Rheinpreussen slag heap, Miner's Lamp by Otto Piene.
Page 2: Grillo Theater, Essen, pages 3–4: Herdecke, railroad viaduct.

Herbe Schönheit zwischen *Lippe* und *Ruhr*

Austere beauty between the Lippe and the Ruhr

Ist das Ruhrgebiet „schön"? Sind stillgelegte Zechen „schön"? Mit der üppig-barocken Pracht süddeutscher Kirchen hat das alles gewiss nichts zu tun. Das Prädikat „schön" wird vermutlich nicht einmal Einheimischen als erstes einfallen: Doch die Monumente einer vergangenen Zeit, die Zechen, Fördertürme, Maschinenhallen faszinieren nicht nur, sie sind auf ihre Art auch schön. Als Stationen auf der Route der Industriekultur gelten sie inzwischen zu Recht als Touristenattraktionen. Sie sind Teil unserer jüngsten Geschichte, denn das, was wir heute „Ruhrgebiet" nennen, gab es vor 150 Jahren noch nicht einmal in Ansätzen. Fast explosionsartig wuchsen kleine, verschlafene Ackerbürgerstädte und Dörfer innerhalb von zwei Generationen zu Großstädten und bildeten das größte industrielle Ballungszentrum Europas. Bis heute erscheint das Gebiet von Duisburg bis Dortmund auf der Landkarte wie eine einzige Megastadt – „Metropole Ruhr". Kohle und Stahl haben regiert. Hier schlug das wirtschaftliche Herz der Bundesrepublik nach dem Zweiten Weltkrieg, von hier aus nahm der wirtschaftliche Aufschwung seinen Anfang. Ganz klar ist das Ruhrgebiet nicht abzugrenzen. Es liegt im Bereich dreier rechter Nebenflüsse des Rheins. Im Norden reicht es bis an die Lippe, den Übergang zum Münsterland. Dazwischen fließt die Emscher, der ungeliebte Abwasserkanal des Reviers, der nach und nach renaturiert werden soll. Im Süden ist es die Ruhr, die Namengeberin des Gebiets.

Is the Ruhr region "beautiful"? Are abandoned coal mines "beautiful"? They are certainly a far cry from the Baroque splendor of the churches of southern Germany. Probably not even the locals would choose the word "beautiful" to describe their native region. But the monuments of a bygone age – the collieries, the winding towers and the machinery sheds – are not just fascinating: they, too, are beautiful in their own way. Today, as "anchor points" along the Industrial Heritage Trail, they are rightfully considered to be a tourist attraction. They are part of our recent history, for the region which we refer to as the "Ruhrgebiet" today hadn't even been thought of 150 years ago. Within the space of just two generations, little agricultrual towns and villages virtually exploded to become big cities, forming the largest industrial conurbation in Europe. To this day, the area between Duisburg and Dortmund appears on the map like a single megalopolis. Coal and steel ruled supreme here. It was here that the economic heart of the Federal Republic beat strongest after World War II; and it was from here that the Economic Miracle gathered momentum. The Ruhr region has no clearly defined borders. It lies around three tributaries on the right bank of the Rhine. In the north it extends as far as the Lippe. In the middle flows the Emscher, the unloved drainage channel of the region which is to be renaturalized in stages. And in the south is the Ruhr, the river which gave the region its name.

Erinpark Castrop-Rauxel – der Park bietet Platz für Gewerbetreibende und ist zugleich ein Naherholungsgebiet. Im Bild zu sehen: die moderne Schmuckfassade eines Gewerbegebäudes.

Erinpark Castrop-Rauxel – the park offers space for businesses and is at the same time an urban recreation area. The photo shows the decorative modern façade of one of the buildings housing businesses.

Lebendiges *Ruhrgebiet* – in den Zechen wird getanzt

The living Ruhr – dancing in the collieries

Dortmund, Zeche Zollern, die Fassade der Waschkaue – in diesem Gebäude haben sich die Bergleute früher nach der Arbeit gewaschen und umgezogen.

Dortmund, Zollern colliery, the façade of the "Waschkaue": It was in this building that the miners washed and changed their clothing after their day's work.

Schmutzig und grau – das war einmal. Der Himmel über dem Revier ist längst wieder blau, nur noch wenige Schlote rauchen und wenn, dann mit neuester umweltfreundlicher Technik. Das Klischee stimmt also längst nicht mehr. Grünflächen und viele Freizeitangebote prägen das neue Bild der Region. Die Megastadt löst sich bei näherem Hinsehen auf in viele kleinere und größere Orte mit je eigenem Flair, eigenem Stolz und eigener Kultur. Mal sind es sportliche Rivalitäten der Fußballvereine, lokale Biermarken oder Traditionen, mit denen das jeweils Eigene gepflegt wird. Das Gemeinsame ist allerdings nicht weniger wichtig: Ein Lebensgefühl, eine Mentalität, die nur hier so gelebt wird und die sich sehr rasch jedem Besucher mitteilt. Die Menchen sind praktisch veranlagt, direkt und unkompliziert. Wer hier zu Besuch ist, fühlt sich gleich willkommen – es sind keine Hürden zu überwinden. Nicht umsonst hat das Ruhrgebiet in den letzten 150 Jahren die wohl gewaltigste Integrationsleistung bewältigt, die je von einer Region gefordert war. In der Solidargemeinschaft der Kumpels haben Tausende von Polen, Italienern, Türken und viele andere Nationalitäten eine neue Heimat gefunden.

Dirty and gray – those times are gone. The sky above the region is blue once more; only a few factory chimneys continue to belch smoke – and if they do, the technology is modern and environmentally friendly. The clichéd image is no longer accurate, then. Green spaces and numerous leisure opportunities characterize the region today. On closer examination the vast conurbation can be divided into a number of towns of various sizes, each with its own atmosphere, local pride and culture. Sometimes rivalry between football clubs, beer brands or traditions provides the feeling of individuality. The sense of community, however, is no less important: an attitude to life, a mentality which can be found only here and which every visitor quickly comes to appreciate. The people here are practical, direct and uncomplicated. Visitors immediately feel the warmth of the welcome. It is not for nothing that during the last 150 years the Ruhr has succeeded in bringing about the most remarkable effort of integration ever demanded of a region. Within the mining community, thousands of Poles, Italians, Turks and other nationalities have found a new home here.

In den Städten existieren heute Kirchen, Moscheen und Synagogen friedlich nebeneinander. Doch im Pott lernten nicht nur die Kulturen miteinander auszukommen, auch eine erste Versöhnung von Arbeit und Kapital fand hier statt: Die Mitbestimmung wurde im Ruhrgebiet erstritten. Einst regierten und lebten die Herren der Zechen und Stahlgießereien wie Fürsten. Sie bauten Fabriken und Schlösser. Sie waren oftmals Patriarchen, durchaus in einem positiven Sinne des Wortes: Sie sorgten zugleich für ihre Arbeiter, ließen Wohnungen, Schulen und Krankenhäuser errichten. Um die Fabriken entstanden „Kolonien", die heute oft unter Denkmalschutz stehen. Von den ursprünglichen Kleinstädten und Dörfern ist wenig übrig geblieben – da und dort eine Altstadt mit Fachwerkhäusern, ein Marktplatz mit Cafés und kleinen Geschäften. Urban ist das Motto des Reviers. An den Wochenenden tobt das Leben, ob im Bermudadreieck in Bochum, in den vielen Klubs, den Theatern, Kinos und Diskotheken. Man feiert, tanzt oder lauscht den Darbietungen von Musikern in stillgelegten Kokereien. Und so ist der Pott heute einer der lebendigsten Landstriche Deutschlands.

In the towns, today you will find churches, mosques and synagogues standing peacefully side by side. In the Ruhr it was not just the different cultures that learned to accept each other; it was here, too, that the first reconciliation of work and capital took place. The right of employees to take part in company policy was fought for, and won, in the Ruhr. The owners of coal mines and steelworks once lived like princes. They built factories and palaces. They were often patriarchs, also in the positive meaning of the word: They took care of their workers, building them homes, schools and hospitals. "Colonies" arose around the factories; many of them are protected buildings today. Little remains of the original small towns and villages – here and there a historic town centre with timbered houses, a market place with cafés and small shops. Otherwise, the region is predominantly urban in character. At weekends everyone is out on the town – in the "Bermuda triangle" in Bochum, and in the numerous clubs, theatres, cinemas and discothèques. The people celebrate, dance or listen to the musical perfomances in the abandoned coking plants. And so, today, the Ruhr is one of the liveliest places of Germany.

Hattingen, Untermarkt und Altes Rathaus.

Hattingen, Untermarkt and Altes Rathaus (Old Town Hall).

An der *Emscher* – von Oberhausen bis Dortmund

On the Emscher – from Oberhausen to Dortmund

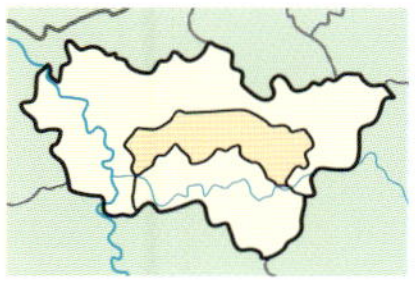

Die Quelle der Emscher liegt südöstlich von Dortmund, bei Dinslaken mündet sie in den Rhein. Der weitgehend eingedeichte Fluss wurde für die Abwasserentsorgung genutzt, was ihm den Namen »Köttelbecke« eintrug. Inzwischen gibt es Klärwerke, und es ist geplant, die Emscher in nächster Zeit wieder zu renaturieren – erste Schritte sind bereits getan. Einige der großen Ruhrgebietsstädte von Oberhausen bis Dortmund liegen in ihrem Bereich.

The source of the Emscher lies south-east of Dortmund; it flows into the Rhine near Dinslaken. Along most of its length, the river flows between embankments. The river was formerly used as a drain, and was hence also known as the "Köttelbecke", or "sewer". Nowadays, there are sewage plants to do the job, and it is planned that the Emscher should be renaturalized in the next few years – indeed, the first steps have already been undertaken. Some of the largest towns of the region lie within its catchment area.

Oberhausen – die Stadt mit dem Gasometer

Oberhausen – the town with the gasometer

Zwei Kabarettistinnen haben vor ein paar Jahren Oberhausen bundesweit bekannt gemacht. Die Missfits tourten mit ihren frechen Sketchen durch ganz Deutschland und besangen ihre Stadt sogar in einem Lied. Manche der Anspielungen haben sich wohl nur Einheimischen gleich erschlossen, so der Spaziergang an der Emscher, dem Abwasserkanal, der bei Ebbe und entsprechender Windrichtung wohl nicht empfehlenswert ist – doch bald soll auch sie keine Abwässer mehr führen. Im Refrain heißt es dann aber mit einem gewissen Stolz: „Steh'n wir auf'm Gasometer in Sturmesbrausen und alles wat de siehst is Oberhausen." Das Gasometer, ein ehemaliger Gasspeicher, ist tatsächlich eines der Wahrzeichen der Stadt. Der mächtige Zylinder dient heute nicht mehr der Speicherung von Gas, sondern ist als Kulturzentrum mit Aussichtsplattform umgebaut. Etwas kritischer sehen die Missfits das *CentrO*, die „Neue Mitte", ein riesiges Einkaufs- und Freizeitzentrum. Zahlreiche Besucher, zum Teil auch aus den Niederlanden, schätzen jedoch längst die vielen Möglichkeiten für Einkauf und Freizeit. Für Kinder ist vielleicht das *SEA-LIFE*-Aquarium interessanter, zumal dort Haie zu sehen sind. Schloss Oberhausen, ein ehemaliger Herrensitz an der Emscher, von dem sich der Name der Stadt ableitet, beherbergt heute eine Galerie. Historisch bedeutsam ist auch die Siedlung Eisenheim, die älteste Arbeitersiedlung des Ruhrgebiets.

A few years ago, two cabaret artists from Oberhausen brought their home town to nation-wide fame. The Missfits toured through Germany with their cheeky sketches and even sang a song about their town. Some of the references were only understood by the locals – such as the walk along the Emscher, the sewer, which is not really to be recommended at low tide and when the wind is blowing in a certain direction. Soon, however, it, too, will no longer be used to carry away effluent. In the refrain, they sang with a certain pride: "When we stand on the gasometer in the height of the storm, Oberhausen stretches as far as we can see." The gasometer, formerly used to store gas, is truly one of the town's main landmarks. Today, the mighty cylinder is no longer used to store gas; it has been turned into a cultural center with an observation platform. Somewhat more critical is the Missfits' attitude toward the *CentrO*, a huge shopping and leisure centre. Nonetheless, large numbers of visitors, some from as far away as the Netherlands, value the wide range of opportunities it offers for shopping and leisure. Children probably find the *SEA-LIFE* aquarium more interesting, especially as you can see some sharks there. Oberhausen Castle, a former aristocratic residence on the Emscher, which gave the town its name, today houses a gallery. Of historic importance is also the Siedlung Eisenheim, the oldest workers' residential complex in the Ruhr.

Seite 12, 13 von links im Uhrzeigersinn: Nordsternpark Gelsenkirchen, Stahlrundbogenbrücke; Fachwerkgehöft im westfälischen Stil in Gladbeck; Dortmund, Fördergerüst der Zeche Zollern; Schloss Bladenhorst, Castrop-Rauxel; Bottrop, Halde Prosper Haniel, Bohrmeißel.

Page 12, 13 clockwise from the left: The arched steel bridge in Nordsternpark, Gelsenkirchen; timbered farmstead in Westphalian style in Gladbeck; Dortmund, winding tower of the Zollern colliery; Bladenhorst Castle, Castrop-Rauxel; boring tool at the Prosper Haniel colliery slag heap, Bottrop.

Von links oben im Uhrzeigersinn: Schloss Oberhausen; Gasometer; Bahnhof im CentrO; Wasserburg Vondern, Stadtbezirk Osterfeld.

Clockwise from top left: Oberhausen Castle; Gasometer; Station at CentrO; Vondern moated castle in the Osterfeld district.

Bottrop – Indoor-Ski und andere Attraktionen

Bottrop – indoor skiing and other attractions

Links: Das Bottroper Tetraeder befindet sich auf den Spitzkegelhalden von Prosper II. Oben: Industriedenkmal Malakow-Turm mit dem Fördergerüst von Prosper II.

Left: The Tetraeder in Bottrop is located on the slag heap of Prosper II. Above: The Malakow Tower, an industrial monument, and the winding tower of Prosper II.

Das „Dorf am Hügel" – so wird der mittelalterliche Name „Borthorpe" gedeutet, aus dem dann Bottrop wurde. 1092 wird die Siedlung erstmals erwähnt. Wahrzeichen der Stadt ist das 1995 errichtete Tetraeder, eine weithin sichtbare Aussichtsplattform aus Stahlrohren. Ungewöhnlich sind einige der Freizeitangebote in Bottrop: Aus der Fülle sei auf das *Alpincenter* mit der längsten Indoor-Skipiste der Welt, den *Movie Park Germany*, ein großer Vergnügungspark im Stadtteil Kirchhellen, und auf das städtische Museum Quadrat hingewiesen. Ein industriegeschichtliches Highlight ist der 1872 errichtete Malakow-Turm der Zeche Prosper II, der besichtigt werden kann.

The medieval name "Borthorpe" is interpreted as meaning "the village on the hill"; it later developed into present-day "Bottrop". The settlement was first mentioned in 1092. The town's main landmark is the Tetraeder, constructed in 1995. This observation platform is made of steel pipes and can be seen for miles around. Some of the leisure facilities in Bottrop are very unusual: they include the *Alpincenter,* with the longest indoor ski slope in the world; the Movie Park Germany, a large amusement park in the Kirchhellen district; and the Quadrat municipal museum. A highlight associated with the region's industrial history is the Malakow Tower at the Prosper II colliery, built in 1872, which is open to the public.

Bottrop – Bauhaus und Bergmannstradition

Bottrop – Bauhaus and mining tradition

Bild aus der Serie „Hommage to the Square“ (1961) von Josef Albers.

Picture from the series "Homage to the Square" (1961) by Josef Albers.

Das „Quadrat“ ist ein Museumskomplex, der sich im Stadtgarten von Bottrop befindet. Der Name bezieht sich einerseits auf die Architektur des 1983 eröffneten Gebäudes mit seinen vier Einzelmuseen, andererseits auf den in Bottrop geborenen Bauhauskünstler Josef Albers (1888–1976) und dessen berühmtesten Bilderzyklus „Hommage to the Square“. Der einflussreiche Farb- und Formtheoretiker ist dank einer Schenkung seiner Witwe mit 85 Gemälden und 250 Grafiken in einem eigenen Trakt vertreten. Zwei andere Teile des Komplexes werden für Wechselausstellungen genutzt. Im vierten Teil ist das Museum für Ur- und Frühgeschichte untergebracht, in dem unter anderem die Skelette eiszeitlicher Tiere, darunter auch ein Mammut, und andere Funde aus dem Emschertal präsentiert werden. Wie es zur Eiszeit in der Gegend um Bottrop ausgesehen hat, wird anschaulich erklärt – hier gab es damals sogar Antilopen. Eine Sammlung von Steinwerkzeugen aus der Urzeit komplettiert die urgeschichtliche Sammlung. Die Ortsgeschichte wird in einem anderen Teil zum Thema – bis zur Industrialisierung war sie überwiegend bäuerlich geprägt.

The "Quadrat" is a museum complex in Bottrop's Stadtgarten park. The name refers, on the one hand, to the architecture of the building, opened in 1983 and containing four separate museums. On the other, it also refers to the Bauhaus artist Josef Albers (1888–1976), who was born in Bottrop, and his most famous picture cycle "Homage to the Square". Albers' theories of color and form were very influential; thanks to a donation by his widow, 85 of his paintings and 250 drawings are displayed in their own section of the museum. Two other sections of the complex are used for changing exhibitions. The fourth section houses the Museum for Prehistoric and Early History, containing the skeletons of Ice Age animals, including a mammoth, and other finds from the Emscher Valley. There are displays clearly showing what the region around Bottrop must have looked like during the Ice Age; there were even antelopes here at the time. A collection of stone tools from earliest times completes the prehistoric collection. Local history is the subject of another section: Until industrialization the region was predominantly agricultural.

Seit 1816 gehörte Bottrop zu Preußen. Der erste Bergbauschacht Prosper I wurde 1856 niedergebracht. Die kleine, ländliche Gemeinde entwickelte sich nun zur Bergbaustadt, in der sich alles um die Kohle drehte. Weitere Zechen kamen hinzu. Die Einwohnerzahl stieg innerhalb zweier Generationen von 4000 auf 72 000, sodass Bottrop 1919 als das „größte Dorf Preußens" galt. Dass das nicht mehr recht zusammenpasste, erkannte man auch in Berlin, der preußischen Hauptstadt. Am 21. Juli 1919 erhob die preußische Staatsregierung den Ort zur Stadt. Kurz nach dem Zweiten Weltkrieg überschritt die Einwohnerzahl erstmals die Schwelle von 100 000. Viele Zechen im Ruhrgebiet sind inzwischen stillgelegt, das Bergwerk Prosper-Haniel in Bottrop ist allerdings noch in Betrieb. Es ist die größte aktive Zeche Deutschlands. Bergleute pflegen ihre Traditionen. Zu festlichen Anlässen wird bis heute die Bergmannsuniform getragen, die schwarze Montur, wie sie sich in Preußen nach 1800 durchgesetzt hat. Typisch ist der Schachthut mit dem Federbusch. Der grüne Federbusch steht für die Sehnsucht des Bergmanns nach der grünen Natur.

Bottop became part of Prussia in 1816. The first mining shaft, called "Prosper I", was sunk in 1856. The little rural community now grew into a mining town, in which everything revolved around coal. More collieries were established. Within two generations, the population expanded from 4,000 to 72,000, so that in 1919, Bottrop was known as the "biggest village in Prussia". Even in Berlin, the capital of Prussia, people realized that the description was no longer appropriate. On July 21, 1919 the government of Prussia elevated the village to the status of town. Not long after World War II, the population surpassed the 100,000 barrier for the first time. Today, many of the collieries in the Ruhr have been closed down; Prosper Haniel mine in Bottrop, however, is still in operation. It is the biggest functional colliery in Germany. Miners preserve their traditions. To this day, the miner's uniform is worn on festive occasions: The black costume became standard in Prussia after 1800. The miner's hat with plume is typical. The green plume symbolizes the miner's yearning for the green pastures of nature.

Bergleute in traditioneller schwarzer Festuniform. Typisch ist der Schachthut mit dem Federbusch.

Miners in traditional black ceremonial uniform. The miner's hat with plume is typical.

Gladbeck – und ein Jahrhundert Kohle

Gladbeck – and a century of coal

Auch der preußischen Landgemeinde Gladbeck wurde – wie Bottrop – erst am 21. Juli 1919 das Stadtrecht verliehen. Doch frühgeschichtliche Funde belegen, dass die Gegend bereits vor 4000 Jahren besiedelt war. Um 900 wird der Ort erstmals schriftlich erwähnt; in einem Güterverzeichnis des Klosters Werden ist von „Gladbeki" die Rede, Besitztümern, die dem Kloster geschenkt worden waren. Bis ins späte 19. Jahrhundert hinein war der Ort ein kleines westfälisches Dorf. Als ab 1878 Kohle gefördert wurde, stieg die Bevölkerungszahl sprunghaft – 1915 waren es bereits über 50 000 Einwohner. Nach dem Zweiten Weltkrieg boomte der Kohlebergbau eine Zeit lang und mit ihm die Stadt, doch ein Ende war bereits absehbar. 1971, nach knapp 100 Jahren, war die Bergbauepoche mit der Schließung der Zeche Graf Moltke zu Ende. Gladbeck hat mit dem notwendigen Strukturwandel bis heute zu kämpfen. Ein Wahrzeichen Gladbecks ist das Schloss Wittringen, ein Wasserschloss, als dessen erster Besitzer 1394 Heinrich von Brachtbecke, „von Wittringe" genannt, erwähnt wird. Nach vielen Wechseln gelangte das Areal 1922 in den Besitz der Stadt Gladbeck, die das Schloss nach alten Plänen im Stil der niederrheinischen Renaissance rekonstruieren ließ. In dem Fachwerkbau neben dem Schloss ist seit 1928 das Museum der Stadt Gladbeck untergebracht. Das Schloss selbst beherbergt heute ein Restaurant.

The rural Prussian community of Gladbeck was awarded municipal rights, like Bottrop, on 21 July 1919. But prehistoric finds prove that the region was already settled 4,000 years ago. The place was mentioned for the first time in written records in 900; a property inventory of Werden Monastery refers to "Gladbeki", which was the name of some properties donated to the monastery. Until the late 19th century, Gladbeck was just a little Westphalian village. After coal began to be mined here in 1878, the population increased rapidly: by 1915 there were no fewer than 50,000 inhabitants. For a time after World War II, coal mining boomed and with it the town, but the end was already in sight. In 1971, after almost 100 years, the mining era came to an end with the closing of the Graf Moltke colliery. To this day, Gladbeck is still struggling with the resultant structural change. One of Gladbeck's main landmarks is Wittringen Castle, a moated building whose first owner was listed in 1394 as Heinrich von Brachtbecke, "von Wittringe". After changing hands many times, the estate finally passed to the town of Gladbeck in 1922. The new owners had the castle rebuilt according to contemporary plans in the style of the Lower Rhine Renaissance. Since 1928 the timbered building beside the castle has housed the municipal museum of Gladbeck. The castle itself today houses a restaurant.

Das Wasserschloss Wittringen mit seinem Hauptgebäude (rechts) und dem Fachwerkbau, in dem heute das Museum der Stadt Gladbeck untergebracht ist.

Moated Wittringen Castle with its main building (right) and the timbered building, which today houses the municipal museum of the town of Gladbeck.

„Zu wissen, worum es wirklich geht. Wie die Bergleute unter Tage. Man muss miteinander klarkommen, darum geht es.“ *Armin Rohde, in Gladbeck geborener deutscher Schauspieler*

“To know what is really important. Just like the miners below ground. They just have to get along with each other. That’s the point.” *Armin Rohde, German actor, born in Gladbeck*

Gelsenkirchen
im Herzen des Reviers …

Gelsenkirchen at the heart of the region …

Wissenschaftspark Gelsenkirchen: Das 300 Meter lange Glasgebäude wird nachts effektvoll beleuchtet. Mehrere Bürotrakte befinden sich darin.

Wissenschaftspark (Science Park) Gelsenkirchen: The glass building, which is 300 metres (984 feet) long, is impressively illuminated at night. It houses a number of office complexes.

Das Motto von Gelsenkirchen lautet „Herz im Revier voll Kraft und Zauber". In ihrer heutigen Gestalt ist die Stadt Ergebnis einer Reihe von Gebietsreformen, durch die mehrere Gemeinden und Städte im Laufe der Zeit zusammengelegt wurden. Als die Schwerindustrie noch in Blüte stand, trug Gelsenkirchen auch den Beinamen „Stadt der 1000 Feuer", wegen der vielen Fackeln im Stadtgebiet, über die das beim Bergbau anfallende Grubengas – im wesentlichen Methan – abgefackelt wurde. Wie viele der heutigen Ruhrgebietsstädte war auch Gelsenkirchen im 19. Jahrhundert noch ein kleiner agrarisch geprägter Ort. Nach der Entdeckung des „schwarzen Goldes" entwickelte sich der Ort sehr rasch zu einem der Zentren der Schwerindustrie. Stadtrechte erhielt Gelsenkirchen 1875. Aus dem Städtchen, das noch 1871 kaum 8000 Seelen zählte, war bereits 1903 eine Großstadt mit fast 140 000 Einwohnern geworden. Bis zum Zweiten Weltkrieg hatte sich die Einwohnerzahl noch einmal mehr als verdoppelt: Wie im ganzen Revier so lag dies auch hier am Zuzug von Menschen aus Ost- und Westpreußen sowie Polen, Arbeitskräfte, die die Industrie dringend brauchte.

Gelsenkirchen's motto is "Our heart in the region full of strength and charm". In its present form the town is the result of a series of territorial reforms which resulted in a number of communities and towns being amalgamated over the years. During the golden age of heavy industry, Gelsenkirchen's nickname was also "the town of 1,000 fires", because of the numerous flames within the area, via which the colliery gas produced during the mining process, mostly methane, was burned off. Like many of the towns in the present Ruhr region, during the 19th century Gelsenkirchen was still just a small farming community. After the discovery of "black gold", it quickly expanded to become one of the centres of heavy industry. Gelsenkirchen was awarded municipal rights in 1875. By 1903, the little town, which in 1871 had a population of scarcely 8,000, had become a big city with almost 140,000 inhabitants. Until World War II, the population had more than doubled again: as in the entire region, this was due to the arrival of people from East and West Prussia and Poland, workers who were badly needed to man the local industry.

Nach dem Zweiten Weltkrieg, in den ersten Boomjahren, waren es vor allem Südeuropäer und Türken, die die Einwohnerzahl nochmals auf fast 390 000 explodieren ließ. Am 17. Dezember 1953 nahm hier die Kokerei Hassel als erste Kokerei nach dem Krieg wieder den Betrieb auf. Mit der Schließung der Zechen erloschen die „1000 Feuer", die Stadt musste sich neu erfinden. Heute sind Forschung und Dienstleistung die größten Arbeitgeber. Auf dem Gelände eines ehemaligen Gussstahlwerks im Stadtteil Ückendorf wurde ein 300 Meter langes Glasgebäude mit Büros errichtet, auf dessen Dach ein Solarkraftwerk für Energie sorgt. Angesiedelt haben sich hier vornehmlich Unternehmen und Forschungseinrichtungen der Energie- und Informationstechnik. Auch Teile der stillgelegten Zechen wurden kreativ umfunktioniert. Das Gebäude mit den Lüftermaschinen der Zeche Consolidation im Stadtteil Bismarck dient heute als Spielstätte mit Schwerpunkt Kinder- und Jugendtheater. Ein besonderer Anziehungspunkt ist auch der Nordsternpark auf dem Gelände der gleichnamigen Zeche, die 1993 stillgelegt wurde.

During the first boom years after World War II, it was primarily southern Europeans and Turks who helped the population to expand until it reached almost 390,000. On 17 December 1953, the Kokerei Hassel went into operation, billed as Germany's "first new coking plant" since the war. When the collieries closed, the "1000 fires" were extinguished and the town had to re-invent itself. Today, research and services are the main sources of employment. On the site of a former cast steelworks, in the Ückendorf district of town, a 300-metre-long (984 feet) glass office building was erected. A solar power station on the roof provides electricity. The companies which have congregated here are mostly firms and research institutes in energy and information technology. Parts of the disused collieries have also been transformed in a creative way. The building which housed the ventilating machines at the Consolidation colliery in the Bismarck district serves today as a theatre where plays for children and young people are mostly presented. A particular attraction is the Nordsternpark on the site of the colliery of the same name, which was decommissioned in 1993.

Das Consol Theater angestrahlt: Hier werden Stücke für Kinder und Jugendliche aufgeführt.

The Consol Theatre in the spotlight: Plays for children and young people are performed here.

… eine Stadt des Fußballs: der *FC Schalke 04*

… a football town: FC Schalke 04

Fast jede Stadt im Ruhrgebiet hat einen eigenen Fußballklub. Zu den bedeutendsten Mannschaften zählt neben Borussia Dortmund der Gelsenkirchener Traditionsverein Schalke 04. Seit 1934 war Schalke 04 siebenmal deutscher Meister, 1997 siegte er im UEFA-Cup. Von den Mitgliederzahlen her ist Schalke einer der größten Sportvereine Deutschlands – über 78 000 Mitglieder sind eingeschrieben, wobei im Verein neben Fußball auch andere Sportarten wie Basketball, Handball und Leichtatletik gepflegt werden. Die „Königsblauen“ tragen seit 2001 ihre Heimspiele in der Veltins-Arena aus, einem der modernsten Stadien der Welt. „Wir geben Gas“ ist durchaus zweideutig, der Hauptsponsor kommt aus Russland und schreibt Gas mit „z“. Der Stadtteil Schalke, ein ehemaliges Industriedorf, das 1903 Gelsenkirchen eingemeindet wurde, ist Namensgeber des Vereins, der dort 1904 gegründet wurde. Zunächst war er ein Zusammenschluss von 14-, 15-jährigen Jungen, die einfach Fußball spielen wollten und sich den Namen „Westfalia Schalke“ gaben. 1909 ließ sich der Verein ins Vereinsregister eintragen. In der 1963 gegründeten Bundesliga war Schalke 04 jahrelang durchgehend vertreten – oft auf dem undankbaren zweiten Tabellenplatz. In den 1980er Jahren stieg der Verein allerdings infolge eines Bestechungsskandals ab. 1991 begann der Wiederaufstieg, der dann 1997 mit dem UEFA-Pokal, dem Auswärtssieg über Inter Mailand, gekrönt wurde.

Virtually every town in the Ruhr has its own soccer club. Apart from Borussia Dortmund, one of the most important teams is the long-standing Gelsenkirchen club, Schalke 04. Since 1934, Schalke 04 has been German champion seven times; in 1997 it won the UEFA Cup. As regards sheer numbers, Schalke is one of the biggest sports associations in Germany, with over 78,000 registered members, although other sports such as basketball, handball and field athletics are practiced in the club, in addition to soccer. Since 2001 the “Royal Blues” have played their home matches in the Veltins Arena, one of the most modern arenas in the world. Their motto, “We step on the gas”, has a double meaning: the team’s main sponsor comes from Russia and spells gas with a “z”. The Schalke district of town, a former industrial village which was amalgamated with Gelsenkirchen in 1903, gave its name to the club, which was founded there in 1904. Initially it was an association of 14- and 15-year-old boys who simply wanted to play soccer and who assumed the name “Westfalia Schalke”. In 1909, the club was registered officially. For years Schalke 04 was represented in the Federal Football League, founded in 1963 – often occupying a thankless second place. In the 1980s, however, the club was relegated following a bribery scandal. The climb back into the top division began in 1991; the ascent was crowned in 1997 with the UEFA Cup in an away victory over Inter Milan.

Das Heimstadion von Schalke 04, die über 60 000 Zuschauer fassende Veltins-Arena ist fast immer ausverkauft. Auf der Tausend-Freunde-Mauer sind die Namen privater Sponsoren festgehalten.

The home stadium of Schalke 04, the Veltins Arena with a capacity of over 60,000 spectators, is almost always sold out. The names of private sponsors are recorded on the “Thousand Friends’ Wall”.

VELTINS ARENA
VELTINS ARENA
Tausend - Freunde - Mauer
VELTINS

Recklinghausen und die Ruhrfestspiele

Recklinghausen and the Ruhr Festival

Links: Recklinghausen Altstadt. Ganz oben: eine typische Küche der 1950er-Jahre, Museum Umspannwerk. Darunter: Rathaus; Haus Reitzenstein.

Left: The historic town centre of Recklinghausen. Above: A typical 1950s kitchen, Museum Umspannwerk. Below: Town Hall; Haus Reitzenstein.

Erstmals schriftlich erwähnt wird Recklinghausen zu Beginn des 11. Jahrhunderts. Stadtrechte wurden dem Ort 1236 verliehen. Im 14. Jahrhundert trat Recklinghausen der Hanse bei und entwickelte sich zu einem Handelszentrum für Tuche und Schmiedewaren. Zur Großstadt avancierte der Ort in den 1950er-Jahren, in den Zeiten des Kohle- und Stahlbooms. Überregional bekannt ist die Stadt durch die jährlichen Ruhrfestspiele, eines der europaweit größten Theaterfestivals. Im alten Umspannwerk in Recklinghausen-Süd ist das „Museum Strom und Leben" untergebracht. Thema ist die Elektrizität, wie sie entdeckt wurde, erst als Luxusgut nur wenigen zur Verfügung stand und heute zum Allgemeingut geworden ist.

Recklinghausen was first mentioned in records during the early 11th century. The town was awarded municipal rights in 1236. During the 14th century, Recklinghausen joined the Hanseatic League and developed into a trading centre for cloth and metal goods. It expanded to become a large town in the 1950s, during the period of the coal and steel boom. The town is famous for the annual Ruhr Festival, one of the biggest drama festivals in Europe. The "Museum Strom und Leben" (Museum of Power and Life) is housed in the old transformer station in south Recklinghausen. The subject is electricity: how it was discovered, was first a luxury commodity, and is now generally available.

Special | Kumpel, Kohle und die Tradition

Miners, coal and tradition

Nach dem Wirtschaftswunder – die Krise

Abgestorbene Pflanzenreste bilden die Grundlage aller Kohlevorkommen der Erde. Über Jahrmillionen wird daraus Torf, dann Braunkohle und schließlich Steinkohle, wobei der Wasseranteil weiter ab- und der Kohlenstoffgehalt stetig zunimmt. Beim Übergang von der Braun- zur Steinkohle spielen Hitze und Druck eine große Rolle. Etwa 100 Kohleflözschichten, jede bis zu drei Meter dick, liegen unter dem Ruhrgebiet übereinander, jeweils getrennt durch andere Gesteinsschichten. Bereits im 13. Jahrhundert wurde nach Kohle gegraben, von Bergbau kann man allerdings erst ab Anfang des 19. Jahrhunderts reden. Damals setzte die Industrialisierung ein, die ab Mitte des Jahrhunderts an Dynamik gewann. Der Steinkohleabbau erfolgte unter Tage. Oberirdisch wurden zahlreiche Fördertürme errichtet, die Kumpel und Maschinen 1000 Meter tief ins Erdinnere beförderten. Viele dieser Türme sind heute Industriedenkmäler. Unter Tage besteht ein Bergwerk aus einer Vielzahl von Tunneln, Strecken genannt, die sich oft über mehrere Quadratkilometer ausdehnen. Der Steinkohlebergbau ist harte Knochenarbeit und oft auch gefährlich. Traditionell ist er Männern vorbehalten. Einheimische Arbeitskräfte reichten schon bald nicht mehr aus. Zigtausende Männer mit ihren Familien wanderten zu und fanden Arbeit, meist kamen sie aus Osteuropa; später folgten die Südeuropäer. Ende der 1950er-Jahre erreichte die Zahl der im Steinkohlebergbau beschäftigten Arbeitnehmer mit über 600 000 einen absoluten Höhepunkt. Damals wurden jährlich über 150 Millionen Tonnen gefördert. Am „Wirtschaftswunder" der noch jungen Bundesrepublik hatte das Revier einen entscheidenden Anteil. Die Kohle- und Stahlkrise setzte 1957/1958 ein, nach und nach mussten viele Zechen schließen. Heute sind nur noch etwa 35 000 Kumpel beschäftigt, die jährlich etwa 21 Millionen Tonnen fördern. Über drei Viertel dieser Menge gehen an die Stromerzeuger, ein Viertel wird zu Koks weiterverabeitet und in der Stahlindustrie eingesetzt. Der Steinkohlebergbau wird subventioniert, weil er heute nicht mehr konkurrenzfähig ist. Es ist billiger, Kohle, Gas und Öl zu importieren. 2018 laufen diese Subventionen aus. Das Kapitel Bergbau im Ruhrgebiet ist dann nach 150 Jahren abgeschlossen. Die Tradition wird im Revier dennoch immer lebendig bleiben.

Arbeitskleidung und Bergleute. Rechts: Fördergerüst Zeche Ewald, Herten.

Working clothes and miners. Right: The winding tower at Ewald colliery, Herten.

After the Economic Miracle – the Crisis

Dead plant matter forms the basis of the world's coal deposits. Over millions of years it was transformed into peat, then into brown coal and finally into mineral coal, whereby the ratio of water sinks and the carbon ratio continuously rises. During the transition from brown coal to mineral coal, heat and pressure are both very important. Some 100 seams of coal, each up to three meters (10 feet) thick, lie on top of each other beneath the Ruhr region, separated from each other by layers of rock. As early as the 13th century, people started digging for coal, but mining as we know it actually dates from the early 19th century. That was when industrialisation began, gaining in momentum from mid-century. Coal mining was carried out underground. At ground level winding towers were erected which carried the miners and their machinery 1,000 meters (3,280 feet) down towards center of the earth. Many of these towers are industrial monuments today. Below ground a mine consists of numerous tunnels, which often extend over an area of several square kilometers (miles). The mining of mineral coal is very hard work and often dangerous. Traditionally, only men work as miners. Before long, local labor was unable to meet the demand. Many thousands of men and their families came as immigrants and found work here. Most of them came from eastern Europe, followed later on by the southern Europeans. By the end of the 1950s the number of workers employed in coal mining had reached its zenith, with over 600,000 men involved. In those days over 150 million tonnes of coal were mined every year. The region played a decisive role in the "Economic Miracle" of the young Federal Republic. The coal and steel crisis began in 1957/1958, so that one by one many collieries had to close. Today, only about 35,000 men work as miners, mining about 21 million tonnes every year. More than three-quarters of this quantity goes to electricity generating plants, and one quarter is processed into coke and used in the steel industry. Mineral coal mining is subsidized because it would otherwise not be competitive. It is cheaper to import coal, gas and oil; the subsidies run out in 2018. Then the chapter "Coal Mining" in the Ruhr will finally be closed, after 150 years. In the region, however, the tradition will live on.

Links: Zeche Zollern, Dortmund, der Maschinensaal; Bergarbeitersiedlung Eisenheim, Oberhausen. Rechts: Karfreitagsumzug, Bergleute in Festtagsuniform, Fahne mit St. Barbara, der Schutzheiligen der Bergleute.

Left: Zollern colliery, Dortmund: the machinery hall; Eisenheim miners' village, Oberhausen. Right: Good Friday procession, with miners in ceremonial uniform, flag with St. Barbara, the patron saint of miners.

Herten und *Herne* sowie zwei Wasserschlösser

Herten and Herne and two moated castles

Herten gehört zum Kreis Recklinghausen. Wie viele andere Ruhrgebietsstädte erlebte auch Herten einen Boom aufgrund der Steinkohle, der etwas über 100 Jahre dauerte. Im Frühjahr 2001 fuhr die letzte Schicht in die Hertener Zeche Ewald. Die Stadt hat das Gelände seither saniert und neue Gewerbe und Dienstleistungsunternehmen angesiedelt; Teile der ehemaligen Förderanlagen stehen unter Denkmalschutz und erinnern an die große Zeit der Montanindustrie. Am Rand der Stadt im Stadtpark liegt das historische Wasserschloss, das erstmals 1376 urkundlich erwähnt wurde. Ab 1968 umfassend restauriert zählt es heute zu den schönsten Baudenkmälern Nordrhein-Westfalens. An der Stelle befand sich ursprünglich eine spätgotische Wehranlage, die Ende des 17. Jahrhunderts zu dem Wohnschloss in seiner jetzigen Form umgebaut wurde. Drei massive Ecktürme stammen noch aus dieser frühen Zeit. Im Schloss befindet sich heute ein Café. Herne liegt 13 Kilometer südlich von Herten und ist seit 1975 mit der ehemaligen kreisfreien Stadt Wanne-Eickel vereint. In Wanne-Eickel wollte man durch diesen Zusammenschluss der Eingemeindung zu Bochum entgehen, die im Zuge der Gemeindegebietsreform drohte. Als ein Standort des Emschertal-Museums Herne wird heute das Wasserschloss Strünkede genutzt. Der stattliche Renaissancebau aus dem frühen 17. Jahrhundert gilt als Wahrzeichen der Stadt.

Herten is part of Recklinghausen district. Like many other towns in the Ruhr, Herten also experienced a boom because of the coal, a boom which lasted somewhat longer than 100 years. In spring 2001, the last shift traveled down into the Ewald mine shaft in Herten. Since then, the town has renovated the site and established new businesses and service companies there; parts of the former mining installations are protected and recall the halcyon days of the coal and steel industry. In the Stadtpark on the outskirts of town lies the historic moated castle, which was first mentioned in records in 1376. Fully restored since 1968, it is now one of the most attractive monuments in North Rhine-Westphalia. A late Gothic defense installation originally stood on the site; at the end of the 17th century it was rebuilt as the residential castle in the form we know it today. Three massive corner towers still date from the building's early years. Today there is a café inside the castle. Herne lies 13 kilometers (8 miles) south of Herten. Since 1975 it has been amalgamated with Wanne-Eickel, a town formerly independent of the district administration. The inhabitants of Wanne-Eickel agreed to the union in order to avoid being swallowed up by Bochum, a move threatened during the course of the local government reform. Strünkede is another moated castle, a Renaissance building dating from the early 17th century. It is the town's principal landmark.

Von links im Uhrzeigersinn: Wasserschloss Herten; Herten, Altes Dorf; Herne, Schloss Strünkede; Zeche Unser Fritz, Herne, beherbergt heute ein Heimatmuseum mit alten Straßenbahnen.
.

Clockwise from top left: Herten Castle; Herten, the Old Village; Herne, Strünkede Castle, Unser Fritz Colliery, Herne, now houses a local history museum with old trams.

„Nichts ist so schön wie der Mond von Wanne-Eickel, die ganze Luft ist erfüllt von ewigem Mai ...“ *Schlagertext von 1962*

“There is nothing as lovely as the moon over Wanne-Eickel; the air is filled with eternal May ...” *Pop song lyrics from 1962*

Castrop-Rauxel und *Waltrop* – Römer und Iren

Castrop-Rauxel and Waltrop – the Romans and the Irish

Die Römer hielten in Castrop einen Militärposten – im Namen steckt das lateinische Wort „castra“ für „Lager, Kaserne“; die germanischen Stämme, die hier bis ins 5. Jahrhundert hinein lebten, trieben damals offenbar regen Handel mit den römischen Besatzern. Als „Villa Castrop“ wurde der Ort erstmals 834 urkundlich erwähnt. Bis ins späte 19. Jahrhundert war es kaum mehr als ein Dorf. 1926 erfolgte die Zusammenlegung mit Teilen des Amtes Rauxel unter dem Namen Castrop-Rauxel. 1975 wurde im Zuge einer kommunalen Neugliederung die Gemeinde Heinrichenburg Teil der Stadt. Der Rhein-Herne-Kanal verbindet Castrop-Rauxel mit den anderen deutschen Wasserstraßen. In Waltrop ist als Industriedenkmal das ehemalige Schiffshebewerk Henrichenburg von besonderer Bedeutung. 1899 von Wilhelm II. feierlich eingeweiht ist es das größte Bauwerk am Dortmund-Ems-Kanal. Mit diesem gigantischen Aufzug konnten Schiffe die 14 Meter hohe Kanalstufe in weniger als drei Minuten überwinden. Heute ist es nicht mehr in Betrieb und Teil eines Museumskomplexes, in dem Besucher erfahren, wie Binnenschiffer früher gelebt haben.

The Romans built a military outpost in Castrop: the very name is based on the Latin word “castra”, meaning “camp, barracks”. The Germanic tribes who lived here until well into the 5th century evidently engaged in lively trading with the Roman occupying forces. The settlement is mentioned for the first time in records in 834, as “Villa Castrop”. Until the late 19th century, it was hardly more than a village. In 1926 it was joined together with part of the official district of Rauxel and was henceforth known as Castrop-Rauxel. In 1975, during a re-organization of district boundaries, the community of Heinrichenburg became part of the town. The Rhein-Herne Canal links Castrop-Rauxel with the other German waterways. Of particular importance in Waltrop is the former ship lift at Henrichenburg. Inaugurated in 1899 by Wilhelm II in a formal ceremony, it is the largest construction on the Dortmund-Ems Canal. With this enormous lift, ships could be raised across the 14-metre-high (46 feet) height difference in less than three minutes. Today, it is no longer in use and is part of a museum complex which provides visitors with a glimpse of how sailors on the country’s inland waterways lived in former times.

Durch das Schiffshebewerk Henrichenburg konnten bis zu 600 Tonnen schwere Frachtschiffe die 14 Meter hohe Kanalstufe überwinden.

The Henrichenburg ship lift enabled freight ships weighing up to 600 tonnes to cross the 14-metre (46-feet) difference in elevation on the canal.

Das 1954 gebaute Fördergerüst von Schacht 7 der Zeche Erin ist heute Wahrzeichen der Stadt.

Today the winding tower structure of Shaft at Erin Colliery 7, built in 1954, is the town's main landmark.

Die Zeche Erin in Castrop-Rauxel war eines der letzten Steinkohlebergwerke, die stillgelegt wurden. Sie wurde 1867 von dem Iren William Thomas Mulvany in Betrieb genommen, der ihr, in Erinnerung an seine Heimat Irland – gälisch „Éire" – den latinisierten Namen „Erin" gab. In den 1870er-Jahren ereigneten sich einige folgenschwere Schlagwetterexplosionen mit Todesopfern, und wegen Wassereinbrüchen musste die Förderung immer wieder eingestellt werden. Die Besitzer wechselten, die Zeche wurde ausgebaut und weitergeführt. 1980 förderte sie mit etwa 2900 Beschäftigten jährlich 1,4 Millionen Tonnen Kohle und erzeugte 640000 Tonnen Koks. Nach 1983 wurden die stillgelegten Schächte verfüllt, als Industriedenkmale sind die Fördertürme über den Schächten 7 und 3 erhalten, das Areal wurde zum Erinpark umgestaltet. Das 1954 in Betrieb genommene Fördergerüst über Schacht 7 ist heute Wahrzeichen der Stadt. Um den Hammerkopfturm von 1920, dem ehemaligen Luft- und Personenbeförderungsschaft der Zeche, ist in Erinnerung an den irischen Gründer ein keltischer Baumkreis gepflanzt.

Erin colliery in Castrop-Rauxel was one of the last of its kind to be decommissioned. It was inuagurated in 1867 by William Thomas Mulvany from Ireland. In memory of his homeland, he gave it the name " Erin", the Latinized version of the Gaelic "Éire". During the 1870s, there were a number of severe explosions of firedamp with fatal results, and mining operations had to be stopped repeatedly because of flooding. The mine changed owners, the colliery was extended and coal extraction continued. In 1980, the mine had approximately 2,900 employees and produced 1.4 million tonnes of coal and 640,000 tonnes of coke per year. After 1983, the shafts which had been closed down were filled in; the winding towers above shafts no. 7 and no. 3 remain as industrial monuments and the site has been remodeled as Erinpark. Today, the winding tower above shaft no. 7, which went into operation in 1954, is the town's main landmark. A Celtic circle of trees has been planted around the hammerhead tower of 1920, the mine's former ventilation and staff transportation shaft, in memory of its Irish founder.

Dortmund – Hansestadt zwischen Bier und Fußball

Dortmund – Hanseatic City between beer and football

Borussia und Bier – das sind die beiden großen Leidenschaften, die die größte Stadt des Ruhrgebiets prägen. Der Fußballverein Borussia Dortmund, der 2009 sein 100-jähriges Jubiläum feiern konnte, belegt seit Jahren stets vordere Tabellenplätze in der Bundesliga. In der höchsten deutschen Spielklasse konnten die Borussen 1994/1995, 1995/1996 und 2001/2002 die Meisterschaft erringen. Heimspiele finden im Westfalenstadion statt, mit seinen über 80 000 Plätzen die größte Fußballarena Deutschlands. Obwohl nur noch wenige der ursprünglich zahlreichen Brauereien überlebt haben, zählt die Stadt doch zu einem der größten Bierproduzenten Deutschlands. Dortmund kann auf eine über 1100-jährige Geschichte zurückblicken. Eine Blütezeit erlebte die Stadt im 14. Jahrhundert als Mitglied der Hanse und als Freie Reichsstadt. Vom 19. bis in die Mitte des 20. Jahrhunderts fällt die zweite Blütezeit: Dortmund war das Zentrum der Industrialisierung im Ruhrgebiet. Weite Teile der Stadt waren nach dem Zweiten Weltkrieg zerstört, doch die Zechen und Hochöfen im Stadtgebiet wurden bald wieder in Betrieb genommen. Die Krise von Kohle und Stahl, die das ganze Ruhrgebiet erfasste, traf jedoch auch Dortmund mit aller Härte. Inzwischen haben sich die wirtschaftlichen Gewichte in Richtung Dienstleistung und Handel verschoben. Dortmund erweist sich heute als eine gastfreundliche Stadt mit vielen kulturellen Angeboten und einer lebendigen Kneipenszene.

Borussia and beer – those are the two great passions of the largest city in the Ruhr region. Borussia Dortmund Football Club, which celebrated its 100th anniversary in 2009, has consistently occupied one of the top places in the league table of the Federal German Football League. Borussia's players even won the championship in the German top division in 1994/1995, 1995/1996 and 2001/2002. Home games take place in the Westfalenstadion, the largest soccer arena in Germany with room for over 80,000 spectators. Although only a few of the originally numerous breweries have survived, the town is also one of the largest beer producer in Germany. Dortmund can look back on over 1,100 years of history. It experienced a golden age in the 14th century as a member of the Hanseatic League and a Free Imperial City. The second boom was during the 19th century, continuing until the middle of the 20th century: Dortmund was the center of industrialisation in the Ruhr. Large areas of the town were destroyed during World War II, but the collieries and furnaces within the city boundaries were soon back in operation. The coal and steel crisis, which affected the entire Ruhr region, also hit Dortmund hard. Since then, the economic balance has shifted towards services and trade. Today, Dortmund is a hospitable city with a wide range of cultural attractions and a lively bar scene.

Von unten links im Uhrzeigersinn: Straßencafé am Europabrunnen in der Fußgängerzone; das im Stil der Neorenaissance 1899 errichtete Alte Rathaus; das Alte Hafenamt beherbergt heute eine Ausstellung über die Schifffahrt.

Right page clockwise from below left: pavement café in pedestrian zone near the "Europa Brunnen" ("Europa Fountain"); the Old Town Hall, built in 1899 in the Neorenaissance style; today the Altes Hafenamt houses an exhibition about shipping.

„Borussia ist Heimat. Das ist das Ruhrgebiet. Das ist das Lebensgefühl der Leute."
Dietmar Bär, Schauspieler, geboren in Dortmund, Borussia-Fan

"Borussia is home. That is the Ruhr. That is the way the people see life here."
Dietmar Bär, actor, born in Dortmund, Borussia Fan

Dortmund, die Zeche Zollern ...

Dortmund, Zollern colliery ...

Die Zeche Zollern, das Gebäude der Alten Verwaltung mit Zinnenkranz und Ecktürmchen, eingerahmt von zwei Fördertürmen.

Zollern colliery, the old administrative building with merlons and corner turrets, framed by two winding towers.

Im Nordwesten Dortmunds im Stadtteil Bövinghausen befindet sich das stillgelegte Steinkohlebergwerk Zeche Zollern II/IV, das zwischen 1898 und 1904 als Musterzeche der Vereinigten Stahlwerke erbaut wurde. Die Zeche besteht aus zwei unter Tage zusammenhängenden Schachtanlagen. Berühmt ist vor allem die Maschinenhalle mit ihrem Jugendstileingang. Heute ist die Zeche Hauptsitz und zugleich einer der Standorte des westfälischen Industriemuseums und ein Ankerpunkt der Europäischen Route der Industriekultur. Die Räumlichkeiten werden auch regelmäßig für Konzertveranstaltungen genutzt. In unmittelbarer Nachbarschaft befindet sich die im Stil des Historismus 1904 erbaute „Kolonie Landwehr“.

In the Bövinghausen district in the northwest of Dortmund, stands the decommissioned mineral coal mine Zollern II/IV, built as a model colliery by the Vereinigte Stahlwerke between 1898 and 1904. The colliery consists of two shaft complexes linked together underground. The most famous feature is the machinery hall with its Art Nouveau entrance. Today the colliery is the headquarters and one of the locations of the Industrial Museum of Westphalia and one of the main anchor points along the European Industrial Heritage Trail. The space is often used for concerts. Nearby is the "Kolonie Landwehr", built in 1904 in historicist style.

... Kultur und Zeugen der *Geschichte*

... Culture and witness of history

Dortmund verfügt über einen Stadthafen – hier beginnt der Dortmund-Ems-Kanal –, eine Universität, Spielstätten für Schauspiel, Oper und Ballett sowie zahlreiche Museen. Neben der Zeche Zollern II/IV können Besucher auch in der 1992 stillgelegten Kokerei Hansa Eindrücke über die frühere Schwerindustrie gewinnen. Wer sich für moderne Kunst interessiert, sollte das 1947 gegründete Museum am Ostwall besuchen. Eine umfangreiche Sammlung von Gemälden der Künstlergruppe „Die Brücke", aber auch Werke aus jüngster Zeit sind zu besichtigen. In einem Art-déco-Gebäude befindet sich das Museum für Kunst- und Kulturgeschichte mit zahlreichen Exponaten zur Geschichte der Stadt. Originell ist das Deutsche Kochbuchmuseum, besonders sehenswert die Sammlung zum Thema Ess- und Tischkultur des 19. Jahrhunderts. Neben vielen anderen Spezialmuseen – zu Themen wie Magnete, Giraffen, Nahverkehr und vieles mehr – dürfen die beiden großen „B"s natürlich nicht fehlen. Das Thema Bier wird im Brauereimuseum anschaulich entfaltet, und das Borusseum an der Nord-Ost-Ecke des Signal-Iduna-Parks zeigt Exponate rund um die Geschichte des Fußballvereins.

Dortmund has a river port – it marks the start of the Dortmund-Ems canal –, a university, theatres for drama, opera and ballet and a number of museums. Apart from Zollern II/IV colliery, visitors can also get an impression of the city's heavy industry in times gone by in the Hansa cokery, closed down in 1992. If you are interested in modern art, you should visit the Museum am Ostwall, founded in 1947. It contains an extensive collection of paintings by the "Die Brücke" artists' association, as well as contemporary works. The Museum of Art and Cultural History presents numerous exhibits relating to the history of the town in an Art-Déco building. The German Cookery Book Museum is an unusual and interesting collection relating to the subject of eating and dining during the 19th century. In addition to numerous other special museums – on subjects including magnets, giraffes, local transport etc. – you should not forget the two "Big Bs". The subject of beer is presented in the Brewery Museum, and the Borusseum on the northeast corner of the Signal-Iduna Park shows exhibits relating to all aspects of the soccer clubs.

Das Museum für Kunst und Kulturgeschichte befindet sich in einem Art-déco-Bau von 1924. Alle Exponate haben Bezug zur Kulturgeschichte Dortmunds.

The Museum für Kunst und Kulturgeschichte (Museum of Art and Cultural History) is housed in an Art Déco building dating from 1924. All the exhibits are linked to the cultural history of Germany.

Im Mittelalter war sie das geistliche Zentrum der Stadt: die St.-Reinoldi-Kirche. Die evangelische Pfarrkirche ist bis heute Mittelpunkt der Stadt und eines ihrer Wahrzeichen. Die dem heiligen Reinoldus, dem Stadtpatron Dortmunds geweihte Kirche, stammt aus dem 13. Jahrhundert. Die Pfeilerbasilika ist spätromanisch, der Chor ist spätgotisch. Die beiden Weltkriege gingen nicht spurlos an der Kirche vorüber. Im Ersten Weltkrieg spendete die Gemeinde die Glocken, das Kupferdach und das Orgelprospekt, das Metall sollte eingeschmolzen und für die Rüstungsproduktion verwendet werden. Im Oktober 1944 wurde die Kirche bis auf die Seitenmauern durch einen Bombenangriff zerstört. Der Wiederaufbau erfolgte in den 1950er-Jahren. Der 104 Meter hohe Kirchturm kann heute bis zur Höhe der ersten Plattform bestiegen werden. Das Geläut besteht aus sechs Glocken, darunter die Dreifaltigkeitsglocke, die mit 6500 Kilogramm schwerste Gussstahlglocke Westfalens. Unter den Kunstschätzen, die meist von Bürgern gestiftet wurden, fällt eine Marienskulptur und das Adlerpult – ein mit einem Bronzeadler geschmücktes Pult, das für die Lesung der Evangelien benutzt wurde –, beide aus dem 15. Jahrhundert, besonders ins Auge.

It was the spiritual heart of the city during the Middle Ages: the Church of St. Reinoldi. The Protestant parish church is the center of the city and one of its landmarks. Dedicated to St. Reinoldus, Dortmund's patron saint, the church dates from the 13th century. The columned basilica is late Romanesque; the choir is late Gothic. The two world wars left their mark on the building. During World War I, the parishioners donated the bells, the copper roof and the organ buffet; the metal was to be melted down and used to produce armaments. In October 1944, the church was destroyed during a bombing raid, after which only the side walls remained. It was rebuilt during the 1950s. The tower of the Reinoldikirche (total height 104 meter/346 feet) can be visited up to the first platform. The heaviest bell weighing 6.5 tonnes is the largest cast steel bell in Westphalia. Among the art treasures, most of them gifts by citizens, the most noteworthy are a statue of the Virgin Mary and the eagle lectern, a reading desk decorated with a bronze eagle used for the reading of the Gospel, both dating from the 15th century.

Der Altar der spätromanischen Reinoldikirche stammt aus der ersten Hälfte des 15. Jahrhunderts.

Folgende Doppelseite: Das Wasserschloss Haus Bodelschwingh wurde im 13. Jahrhundert errichtet und befindet sich bis heute in Familienbesitz.

The altar of St Reinoldi's church dates back to the first half of the 15th century.

Following double page: Haus Bodelschwingh, a moated castle, built in the 13th century and still owned by the family.

Um die *Ruhr* – von Mülheim, über Essen bis Hagen

Around the Ruhr – from Mülheim via Essen to Hagen

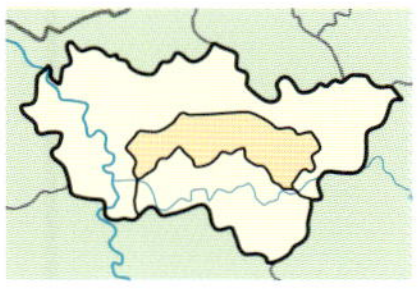

Die Ruhr, ein etwa 220 Kilometer langer rechter Nebenfluss des Rheins, ist Namengeberin der größten Industrieregion Europas. Sie entspringt im Rothaargebirge im Hochsauerland. Früher war sie eine der meist befahrenen Wasserstraßen Deutschlands, heute wird nur der Abschnitt von Mülheim bis zum Rhein für den Gütertransport genutzt. Wirtschaftlich bedeutend ist die Ruhr für die Wasserversorgung der Region. Das Ruhrtal ist außerdem ein beliebtes Naherholungsgebiet.

The Ruhr, a tributary on the right bank of the Rhine, is about 220 kilometres (138 miles) long and has given its name to the biggest industrial region in Europe. The river rises in the mountains of the Rothaargebirge. It was once one of the most heavily used waterways of Germany, but today only the stretch between Mülheim and the Rhine is used for goods transport. The Ruhr is important for the region as a water supply. The Ruhr Valley is also a popular recreational area.

Essen – vom Damenstift zur Grugahalle

Essen – from a convent to the Grugahalle

Archäologische Funde belegen es: Bereits viele Tausend Jahre vor Chr. war die Gegend um Essen besiedelt. Als Keimzelle der heutigen Ruhrmetropole gilt jedoch ein Damenstift, das im 9. Jahrhundert für die unverheirateten Töchter und die Witwen des sächsischen Hochadels gegründet wurde. Bald danach folgte ein erster Kirchenbau, der den Heiligen Cosmas und Damian, den Schutzpatronen der Ärzte und Apotheker, sowie der Jungfrau Maria geweiht war. Das Gotteshaus brannte in der Vergangenheit mehrfach ab, an seiner Stelle steht heute das Münster, die Bischofskirche des Ruhrbistums. Essen bildet den Mittelpunkt der Kulturhauptstadt Europas für 2010, zu der das Ruhrgebiet erklärt wurde. Die Metropole war einst untrennbar mit der Schwerindustrie und dem Namen Krupp verbunden, die Fabriken der Krupp-Werke beschäftigten bereits Ende des 19. Jahrhunderts Zehntausende von Arbeitskräften. Mit der Krise der Montanindustrie begann die Neupositionierung der Stadt. 1972 wurde die Universität gegründet. Essen ist Messestadt – eines der Highlights ist die „Techno-Classica“, die jährlich stattfindende größte Oldtimermesse der Welt. Für Kinofreunde bietet die Lichtburg die größte Kinoleinwand Deutschlands. Das Museum Folkwang verfügt über eine bedeutende Sammlung moderner Kunst. Die Grugahalle mit Platz für bis zu 10 000 Besucher wird für Popkonzerte, Sportveranstaltungen und andere Großereignisse genutzt.

Archeological finds proved that the region around Essen was already settled many thousands of years before our era. However, the nucleus of today's Ruhr metropolis is generally considered to be a convent founded during the 9th century for the unmarried daughters and widows of the Saxon nobility. The first church building followed shortly afterwards, dedicated to Saints Cosmas and Damian, the patron saints of doctors and apothecaries, and the Virgin Mary. The church was burned down on several occasions during its history; the Cathedral, the episcopal church of the bishopric of the Ruhr, now stands on the site. Essen will be the centre of the European Capital of Culture for 2010; the Ruhr region as a whole has been awarded the title. The city was originally inseparably linked with heavy industry and the name of Krupp; by the end of the 19th century, the factories of the Krupp already employed tens of thousands of workers. The crisis in the coal and steel industry coincided with the re-positioning of the city. The university was founded in 1972. Essen is a trade-fair city – one of the highlights is the "Techno-Classica", the largest veteran car fair in the world, which is held every year. For cinema fans, the Lichtburg offers the largest cinema screen in Germany. The Folkwang Museum houses an important collection of modern art. The Grugahalle has space for up to 10,000 spectators and is used for pop concerts, sports events and other major spectacles.

Seite 42 – 43 von links: Weihnachtsmarkt in Essen, links das Münster, in der Mitte das neue Rathaus und im Vordergrund das Reiterdenkmal Wilhelm II. Schloss Broich bei Mülheim a.d.Ruhr. Bochum-Stiepel, Dorfkirche und ältestes Gebäude der Stadt. Ruhrlandschaft bei Witten. Essen, Förderturm, Zeche Zollverein.

Page 42– 43 from left: Christmas market in Essen; the cathedral is on the left, the New Town Hall in the center and the equestrian monument to Wilhelm II in the foreground. Broich Castle near Mülheim an der Ruhr. Bochum Stiepel, the oldest building of Bochum. Ruhr landscape near Witten. Essen, the winding tower of Zollverein colliery.

Von links oben im Uhrzeigersinn: Essen-Werden, St.-Luzius-Kirche, älteste Pfarrkirche nördlich der Alpen; Grugahalle; Synagoge; Kino Lichtburg.

Clockwise from top left: Essen-Werden, Church of St. Luzius, the oldest parish church north of the Alps; the Grugahalle; the Synagogue; Lichtburg cinema.

Essen – Margarethenhöhe und Schloss Borbeck

Essen – Margarethenhöhe and Borbeck Castle

Die Siedlung Margarethenhöhe im gleichnamigen Essener Stadtteil gilt als eine der ersten deutschen Gartenstädte. Gestiftet wurde die Siedlung 1906 von Margarethe Krupp, der Ehefrau des Firmengründers Alfred Krupp. Erbaut wurde die Siedlung nach Plänen des Architekten Georg Metzendorf zwischen 1909 und 1938. Ein Regierungserlass befreite Metzendorf von allen üblichen Bauvorschriften. Mit dem Projekt sollte menschenfreundliches Wohnen verwirklicht werden, günstiger Wohnraum in natürlicher Umgebung, den sich auch weniger Begüterte leisten konnten. In 935 Gebäuden wurden auf etwa 115 Hektar – wovon 50 Hektar als Waldgebiet erhalten bleiben sollte – 3092 Wohneinheiten geschaffen. Die Wohnungen waren klein, aber praktisch geschnitten. Im Zweiten Weltkrieg wurde die Siedlung stark beschädigt. Nach Kriegsende restaurierte man die Häuser wieder in ihrer ursprünglichen Form. Sie stehen seither unter Denkmalschutz. Einfache Arbeiter leben dort nicht mehr, die Siedlung gilt inzwischen als ein bevorzugtes Wohngebiet. Im Essener Ruhrlandmuseum kann eine Musterwohnung besichtigt werden, die im Stil der frühen Jahre eingerichtet ist.

The Margarethenhöhe estate in the district of Essen which bears the same name is considered to be one of the earliest garden towns in Germany. The estate was donated in 1906 by Margarethe Krupp, the wife of Alfred Krupp, the firm's founder. The estate was built according to plans by the architect Georg Metzendorf between 1909 and 1938. An official decree freed Metzendorf from having to comply with all the usual building regulations. The project was designed to create a congenial living environment with inexpensive accommodation for the less-well-off in a natural setting. 3,092 residential units were created in 935 buildings on about 115 hectares (284 acres) – 50 hectares (124 acres) of which were to remain as undeveloped woodland. The apartments were small but practical. During World War II, the estate was badly damaged. The houses were restored to their original state at the end of the war. They are now protected buildings. Unskilled workers no longer live here, however, as the estate has become a sought-after place to live. A model flat, furnished in the style of the early years, can be seen in the Ruhrlandmuseum in Essen.

Das Gasthaus am Markt in der Siedlung Margarethenhöhe, eine der ersten deutschen Gartenstädte, beherbergt heute ein Viersternehotel.

Today, the "Gasthaus" of the Margarethenhöhe estate, one of the first garden towns in Germany, houses a four-star-hotel.

Im Essener Stadtteil Borbeck befindet sich das gleichnamige Wasserschloss, das seit dem 14. Jahrhundert von den Essener Fürstäbtissinnen als Residenz genutzt wurde. Sein heutiges Aussehen erhielt das Gebäude im 18. Jahrhundert. Damals wurde auch der Schlosspark mit seinen Wasserspielen, einer künstlichen Ruine und Volieren angelegt. Die letzte Äbtissin plante noch einen Umbau, doch 1802 wurde die Anlage von Preußen vereinnahmt. Nach der Säkularisation 1803 war das Schloss zunächst im Besitz der preußischen Staats- und Domänenkammer, wurde aber bald wieder verkauft und kam wieder in private Hände. 1941 erwarb schließlich die Stadt Essen die Anlage. In der Nachkriegszeit wurde das Schloss von der Stadtverwaltung benutzt. Heute wird das Gebäude, das seit 1985 unter Denkmalschutz steht, als Kultur- und Begegnungsstätte eingesetzt. Es beherbergt die Folkwang Musikschule und einen Teil der städtischen Volkshochschule. Das Standesamt von Borbeck befindet sich dort, im ehemaligen Wirtschaftsgebäude werden regelmäßig Ausstellungen veranstaltet. Der Residenzsaal wird für Klassik- und Jazzkonzerte genutzt. Der Schlosspark ist frei zugänglich.

Moated Borbeck Castle stands in the district of Essen which bears the same name. From the 14th century, it was used as the residence of the princess-abbesses of Essen. The building's present-day appearance dates back to the 18th century. It was in those days, too, that the palace park was laid out with its fountains, artificial ruins and aviaries. The last abbess planned to rebuild the castle, but it was confiscated by Prussia in 1802. After secularization in 1803, the castle remained initially in the possession of the Prussian Chamber of State and Properties, but it was sold shortly afterwards and returned to private ownership. The City of Essen finally bought the property in 1941. During the postwar years, the castle was used by the town administration. Since 1985, the building has been protected. It is used as a centre for cultural encounters. It houses the Folkwang music school and parts of the city's folk high school. Borbeck Registry Office is also there, and exhibitions are held in the former outbuildings. The hall of the Residence is used for classical and jazz concerts. The castle park is open to the public.

Das Schloss Hugenpoet in Essen-Kettwig steht unter Denkmalschutz und beherbergt heute ein Hotel-Restaurant.

Hugenpoet Castle in Essen-Kettwig is a protected building and houses a hotel-restaurant.

Special | Krupp – eine Essener Industriellendynastie

Krupp – an Essen industrial dynasty

Von den nahtlosen Radreifen …

Unter Alfred Krupp (1812–1887) wurde aus einer Werkstatt in der zweiten Hälfte des 19. Jahrhunderts das größte Unternehmen Europas. Furios der Start mit dem nahtlos geschmiedeten Eisenbahnrad, genau zur rechten Zeit, als weltweit die Eisenbahnen ausgebaut wurden. Und dann kamen die Geschützrohre aus Stahl, die den alten gusseisernen an Präzision und Stabilität überlegen waren. Krupp belieferte Freund und Feind, am Sieg der Deutschen im Deutsch-Französischen Krieg 1870/71 war Kruppstahl mit beteiligt. Alfred wurde als „Kanonenkönig" bezeichnet. Auch die Villa Hügel, 1873 erbaut nach eng mit Alfred abgestimmten Plänen, erwies sich als technische Herausforderung: Das Haus mit seinen 269 Räumen war mit den damaligen Mitteln nicht zu beheizen, die Kinder und Enkel erlebten es als kalt und ungemütlich. 1887 starb der Patriarch. Friedrich Alfred als Erstgeborener übernahm das Ruder, unter Kaiser Wilhelm II. kam es zu massiver Aufrüstung, die Auftragsbücher der Krupp-Fabriken waren voll. Um 1900 waren schon über 45 000 Arbeiter beschäftigt.

From seamless wheels …

During the second half of the 19th century, a workshop grew to become the largest industrial concern in Germany under Alfred Krupp (1812–1887). The company got off to a first-rate start with the seamless railroad wheel, which was invented just in time for the worldwide expansion of the railroad. They were followed by the steel gun barrels, which were superior to the old cast-iron ones. Krupp supplied them to friends and enemies alike; Krupp played a part in the German victory in the Franco-Prussian War of 1870/71. Alfred Krupp became known as the "Kanonenkönig", the "Gun King". The Villa Hügel, built in 1873 in accordance with plans largely by Krupp himself, turned out to be a technical challenge: With its 269 rooms, it was impossible to heat with the systems available at the time, so that his children and grandchildren experienced it as both cold and uncomfortable. The patriarch died in 1887. Friedrich Alfred, the eldest son, took over the command. Under Kaiser Wilhelm II, there was a massive military build-up and the order books of the Krupp factories were full. By 1900, the company already employed over 45,000 workers.

Villa Hügel in Essen; Alfried Krupp von Bohlen und Halbach, der „letzte Krupp“.

Villa Hügel in Essen; Alfried Krupp von Bohlen und Halbach, the “last Krupp”.

… zum größten Rüstungskonzern

1902 starb Friedrich Alfred, kurz nachdem eine Zeitschrift das Gerücht von seiner Homosexualität verbreitet hatte. Ob es Selbstmord war, ist bis heute umstritten. Seine Tochter Bertha, damals gerade 16, war die reichste Erbin Deutschlands. Ein passender Mann wurde gesucht und fand sich 1906 in dem Diplomaten Gustav von Bohlen und Halbach. Erstgeborener aus dieser Verbindung war Alfried (1907–1967). Im Ersten Weltkrieg wurden Waffen aus Kruppstahl eingesetzt. Auch Hitler brauchte Krupp und Krupp brauchte Hitler. Krupp war der wichtigste Rüstungslieferant. 1943 gab Gustav die Leitung an Alfried ab. Mitten im Krieg fehlten Arbeitskräfte, doch die Produktion war für die Nazis kriegswichtig: Zwangsarbeiter wurden beschäftigt, fast 100 000. Nach Kriegsende verurteilte das Nürnberger Tribunal Alfried zu zwölf Jahren Gefängnis. Schon 1951 kam er frei und übernahm bei Krupp wieder das Ruder. Sein Sohn Arndt erwies sich als Nachfolger ungeeignet, weshalb Alfried – selbst schon schwerkrank – 1967 Krupp an eine Stiftung übertrug. Nach 150 Jahren erlosch so der Familienname Krupp. Arndt starb 1986 an Krebs.

… to the biggest armaments concern

Friedrich Alfred died in 1902, shortly after a magazine had spread rumors about his homosexuality. It is a matter of controversy to this day as to whether he committed suicide or not. His daughter Bertha, who was only 16, became Germany's richest heiress. A search for a suitable husband was initiated, and in 1906 the choice fell on the diplomat Gustav von Bohlen und Halbach. Their eldest son was Alfried (1907–1967). Weapons made of Krupp steel were employed during World War I. Hitler also needed Krupp, and Krupp needed Hitler. Krupp was the most important weapons supplier. In 1943, Gustav handed over the direction of the firm to Alfried. By the middle of the war there was a shortage of workers; almost 100,000 forced laborers were employed. At the end of the war, Alfried was sentenced to 12 years' prison at the Nuremberg trials. He was released in 1951, however, and took over the command of the company. His son Arndt proved to be an unsuitable successor, and so Alfried handed over power to a foundation in 1967. After 150 years, the Krupp family name disappeared; Arndt died of cancer in 1986.

Links: Terrasse der Villa Hügel; Statue von Alfred Krupp, unter dem Krupp das größte Industrieunternehmen Europas wurde. Rechts: zwei Sphinxen vor der Villa Hügel.

Left: The terrace of the Villa Hügel; Statue of Alfred Krupp, under whom Krupp became the biggest industrial concern in Europe. Right: Two sphinxes at the Villa Hügel.

Essen Zollverein – die „schönste Zeche der Welt“

Essen Zollverein – the “most beautiful colliery in the world”

Die Zeche Zollverein steht einerseits beispielhaft für den Aufstieg und den Niedergang einer der größten Industrieregionen Europas, andererseits für eine kreative Art, mit dem damit verbundenen Erbe umzugehen. Seit 2002 wird die Zeche Zollverein Schacht XII und die benachbarte Kokerei auf der Liste des UNESCO-Welterbes geführt. Die Zeche geht auf eine Gründung des Industriellen Franz Haniel (1779–1868) zurück. Der Unternehmer suchte nach Steinkohlevorkommen, aus denen Koks für die Stahlproduktion hergestellt werden konnte. Er wurde fündig und benannte die Zeche nach dem 1834 gegründeten Deutschen Zollverein, mit dem erstmals ein Binnenmarkt – wenn auch unter preußischer Vorherrschaft – innerhalb der deutschen Bundesstaaten geschaffen war. Der Name ist Programm: Der industrielle Aufstieg beruhte nicht zuletzt auch auf dem Wegfall vieler Handelsschranken und damit der Schaffung eines großen Binnenmarktes. Ein weiterer Faktor waren die Eisenbahnen, die als neue Verkehrsmittel auf Stahl angewiesen waren. Die erste Steinkohle wurde 1851 gefördert; neben der Schachtanlage nahm 1866 eine Kokerei ihren Betrieb auf.

Zollverein colliery is, on the one hand, a prime example of the rise and fall of one of the great industrial regions of Europe; and, on the other, it also represents a creative way of dealing with the heritage associated with this history. Since 2002, Shaft XII of Zollverein colliery and the neigboring cokery have been included in the UNESCO World Heritage list. The colliery was founded by industrialist Franz Haniel (1779–1868). As a businessman, he needed a supply of coal from which he could produce coke for the manufacture of steel. He found it and named the colliery for the German Zollverein (German Customs Union), founded in 1834, which first created a domestic market – albeit under Prussian rule – within the German federal states. The name was significant: the industrial expansion was due not least to the removal of many trade barriers. A further factor was the railroad, a new form of transport which was dependent upon steel. The first coal was mined here in 1851; a cokery was set up beside the shaft installations in 1866.

Im ehemaligen Kesselhaus befindet sich heute das „red dot design museum“, in dem auf 4000 Quadratmetern preisgekrönte Exponate modernen Designs zu sehen sind.

Today you will find the “red dot design museum” in the former boiler room. Prize-winning exhibits of modern design are displayed over an area of 4,000 square metres (43,040 square feet).

Industriedenkmal und UNESCO-Welterbe: Förderschacht 12 der Zeche Zollverein. Folgende Doppelseite: die effektvoll beleuchtete Maschinenseite der Kokerei.

Industrial monument and a part of the UNESCO Cultural Heritage: Winding tower no. 12 of Zollverein colliery. Following double page: The machinery of the cokery is effectively illuminated.

Das Doppelbockfördergerüst von Schacht 12 wurde 1932 eingeweiht und war in seiner Bauweise Vorbild für viele Förderanlagen. 1961 wurde eine neue Kokerei in Betrieb genommen, die damals als modernste ihrer Art galt: Täglich konnten in ihren 192 Öfen 10 000 Tonnen Kohle zu Koks veredelt werden. Als Ruhrkohle nicht mehr konkurrenzfähig war, wurde im Dezember 1986 auch Schacht 12 stillgelegt; 1993 folgte die Schließung der Kokerei. Das Gelände wurde vom Land Nordrhein-Westfalen gekauft, saniert und unter Denkmalschutz gestellt. Es ist heute eine der zentralen Stationen der Europäischen Route der Industriekultur. Eine Reihe von Museen und ein Museumspfad erschließen nicht nur das Thema Bergbau; ein Schwerpunkt liegt darüber hinaus auf Design und Architektur – das „red dot design museum" im umgebauten Kesselhaus widmet sich der zeitgenössischen Gestaltung von Alltagsprodukten wie Besteck, Möbeln bis zu Fahrzeugen. Ausgestellt werden Objekte, die mit dem jährlich vergebenen „red design award" ausgezeichnet wurden. Das Gelände wird heute außerdem für kulturelle Veranstaltungen wie Konzerte und Ausstellungen genutzt.

The Doppelbock winding tower of shaft 12 was inaugurated in 1932; its construction served as model for many mining installations. In 1961, a new cokery was installed. It was considered the most modern of its kind at the time; in its 192 furnaces it was able to process 10,000 tonnes of coal into coke every day. After Ruhr coal had become no longer competitive, Shaft 12 was decommissioned in December 1986 as well; the cokery was shut down in 1993. The site was purchased by the state of North Rhine-Westphalia, renovated and placed under a protective order. Today, it is one of the central anchor points of the European Industrial Heritage Trail. A number of museums and a museum trail are devoted not only to the subject of mining: another focal point is that of design and architecture – the "red dot design museum" in the converted boiler house is dedicated to the contemporary design of everyday items, such as cutlery and furniture or vehicles. The objects on view have been honored with the annual "red design award". Today, the site is also used for cultural events, such as concerts and exhibitions.

Grüne Stadt am Fluss: *Mülheim an der Ruhr*

The green town by the river: Mülheim an der Ruhr

Mülheim an der Ruhr wurde 1808 zur Stadt erklärt – nach französischem Recht. Die Niederlage Napoleons 1815 bei Waterloo führte zur Neuordnung Europas auf dem Wiener Kongress: Mülheim kam in der Folge zu Preußen. Erst 1846 erhielt Mülheim auch das preußische Stadtrecht. In der zweiten Hälfte des 19. Jahrhunderts wurde die Stadt zu einem Industriestandort: Die erste mit Koks befeuerte Stahlhütte des Ruhrgebiets nahm hier 1849 die Produktion auf. In Styrum bei Mülheim (heute ein Stadtteil) gründete August Thyssen (1842–1926), neben Alfred Krupp einer der „Barone" der Schwerindustrie, 1871 das Walzwerk Thyssen & Co. Der 50 Meter hohe Wasserturm, den Thyssen damals zur Versorgung seiner Stahlwerke anlegen ließ, steht heute unter Denkmalschutz und wurde zum Museum umgebaut. In Mülheim wurde auch Hugo Stinnes (1870–1924) geboren, der nach dem Ersten Weltkrieg einen Riesenkonzern aufgebaut hatte und zu den einflussreichsten Persönlichkeiten des Deutschen Reiches zählte. Nach dem Zweiten Weltkrieg, in dem Mülheim stark zerstört wurde, erlebte die Schwerindustrie ein Zwischenhoch. In den 1960er-Jahren begann auch für Mülheim im Zuge der Stahl- und Kohlekrise der schwierige Strukturwandel. Bereits 1966 wurde in Mülheim als erster Stadt im Ruhrgebiet kein Bergbau mehr betrieben. Heute gilt „die Stadt am Fluss" mit über 50 Prozent Grünflächen als attraktiver Wohnort.

Mülheim an der Ruhr was incorporated as a town in 1808 – according to French law. Napoleon's defeat in 1815 at Waterloo led to the re-ordering of Europe at the Congress of Vienna, during which Mülheim was ceded to Prussia. It was not until 1846 that Mülheim was awarded a town charter according to Prussian law. During the second half of the 19th century, the town became an industrial base: The first steelworks in the Ruhr to be fired with coke began production here in 1849. It was in Styrum bei Mülheim (today a district of the town) that August Thyssen (1842–1926), one of the "Barons" of heavy industry like Alfred Krupp, founded the steel mill Thyssen & Co. in 1871. Thyssen had built a 50-metre-(164-foot) high water tower to provide water for his steelworks; today it is a protected building and has been turned into a museum. It was in Mülheim, too, that Hugo Stinnes (1870–1924) was born; after World War I he built up an enormous company and became one of the most influential personalities in the German Empire. Mülheim was badly damaged during the Second World War; after that heavy industry experienced a temporary boom. During the 1960s the coal and steel crisis Mülheim, too, was forced to undergo a difficult period of structural change. As early as 1966, Mülheim became the first town in the Ruhr to stop mining. Today, the "town by the river" consists of more than 50 percent open spaces and is considered an attractive place to live.

Mülheim Ruhrtalbrücke mit Ausflugsschiff; Fachwerkhäuser in der Altstadt; der Wasserturm Aquarius diente ursprünglich der Versorgung des Stahlwerks, heute ist er zum Museum umgebaut.

Mülheim: Bridge over the Ruhr with excursion ship; timbered houses in the Old Town; the Aquarius water tower originally provided the steelworks with water; today it has been transformed into a museum.

Bochum, vom einstigen Ackerbürgerstädtchen …

Bochum, from former farming town …

Dieser geschnitzte neugotische Flügelaltar befindet sich in der Propsteikirche St. Peter und Paul.

The winged neo-gothic altar can be seen in the Provostry of St Peter and Paul's Church.

Es gibt Städte, die sind nicht eigentlich schön, ihr Charme ist eher herb und für Besucher nicht leicht zu erkennen. Bochum ist eine solche Stadt. Die kreisfreie Universitätsstadt bildet das Zentrum des mittleren Ruhrgebiets. Stadtrechte wurden dem Ort 1321 zugesprochen, und bis 1850 war Bochum ein eher verschlafenes Städtchen mit gerade einmal 5000 Einwohnern, die meisten davon Ackerbürger, also im Ort ansässige Bauern. Der Abbau von Kohle, zunächst im Tagebau, ist schon für das 15. und 16. Jahrhundert belegt, doch die Blütezeit setzte 1832 ein mit dem Übergang vom Tage- zum Untertagebau. Die Zahl der Einwohner hatte sich bis 1895 verzehnfacht, und nur fünf Jahre später noch einmal – zum Teil durch Eingemeindungen – mehr als verdoppelt: Ab 1904 war Bochum Großstadt. Auch Bochum wurde im Zweiten Weltkrieg teilweise zerstört. In der Nachkriegszeit entwickelte sich die Stadt zu einem Kulturzentrum des Ruhrgebiets. Von der einstigen Ackerbürgerstadt ist wenig übrig geblieben: Eines der wenigen Bauwerke aus dieser Zeit ist die Propsteikirche St. Peter und Paul mit ihrem Turm aus dem 14. Jahrhundert und der spätgotischen Halle (im Zweiten Weltkrieg zerstört, bis 1959 wieder aufgebaut).

Some towns cannot really be described as beautiful; their charm is of an austere kind which is not easy for visitors to recognize. Bochum is one of those towns. It is a university town which is independent of the surrounding district, and it forms the heart of the central Ruhr region. It was awarded its municipal charter in 1321, and until 1850 Bochum was a rather sleepy little town with a population of scarcely 5,000, the majority of them farmers. Coal mining, initially as opencast mining, took place here as early as the 15th and 16th century, but its golden age began in 1832 with the transition from opencast to underground mining. The number of inhabitants had increased tenfold by 1895, and just five years later it had more than doubled again, partly through the town's amalgamation with other communities. Bochum began as a metropolis in 1904. The city was partly destroyed during World War II. During the postwar period, the town developed into a cultural centre. Little has remained of the former farming community: one of the few buildings left is the Provostry Church of SS. Peter and Paul with its 14th-century tower and late-Gothic hall (destroyed during World War II and rebuilt in 1959).

Als erste Universitätsneugründung der Bundesrepublik begann hier 1965 die Ruhruniversität ihren Lehrbetrieb. Sie ist mit über 30 000 Studierenden die größte Campusuniversität im Revier und eine der größten Universitäten Deutschlands. Der Campus befindet sich am Rand einer Anhöhe über dem Kemnader See. Unmittelbar neben den Betonbauten der Universität inmitten eines waldreichen Areals im Stadtteil Querenburg bietet der Botanische Garten einen Ruhe- und Erholungsbereich, der tagsüber frei zugänglich ist. Der Garten gehört zur Biologischen Fakultät der Universität und dient zu Studien- und Forschungszwecken. Besonders beliebt ist der im südchinesischen Stil gestaltete, etwa 1000 Quadratmeter große Chinesische Garten, der 1990 als Garten im Garten eingerichtet wurde. Das Refugium erhielt den Namen „Qian Yuan" (Garten Qians), in Erinnerung an den chinesischen Dichter Tao Qian (365–427), der bis heute in China viel gelesen wird. Ein Teich wurde angelegt, Felsenlandschaften und ein Pavillon laden zu meditativem Verweilen ein. Chinesische Fachleute haben als Berater bei der Gestaltung mitgewirkt. Originalmaterialien aus China – Holzelemente, Ziegel – kamen zum Einsatz.

The University of the Ruhr was founded here in 1965 as the first new university in the Federal Republic. With over 30,000 students, it is the biggest campus university in the region and one of the biggest universities in Germany. The campus lies on the edge of a hill overlooking the Kemnader See. Next to the concrete buildings of the university, set in a wooded area in the Querenburg district of town, lies the Botanic Garden, a park for rest and recreation which is open to the public during the daytime. The garden belongs to the Faculty of Biology of the university and is used for study and research purposes. The Chinese Garden, covering an area of some 1,000 square meters (10,760 square feet) and laid out in 1990 in the south Chinese style, is particularly popular. This oasis of calm was named "Qian Yuan" (Qian's Garden) in honor of the Chinese poet Tao Qian (365–427 A.D.). It includes a pond, a rocky landscape and a pavilion which invites the visitor to meditation. The garden was designed with the assistance of Chinese experts and makes use of original materials from China, such as wooden elements and tiles.

Der Chinesische Garten ist ein besonders beliebter Teil des Botanischen Gartens der Universität Bochum.

The Chinese Garden, a very popular section of the Botanic Garden of Bochum University.

… zur Theater- und *Kulturmetropole*

… to theatrical and cultural metropolis

Bochum ist eine Stadt der Museen. Unter den zwölf Museen ragt das Deutsche Bergbaumuseum als Zentrum der Montangeschichtsforschung heraus. Unübersehbar ist der Förderturm der ehemaligen Zeche Germania, der 1974 in Dortmund abgebaut und in Bochum wieder aufgebaut wurde und der inzwischen zu einem Wahrzeichen der Stadt avanciert ist. Das Museum ist das größte seiner Art in der Welt. Neben vielen Exponaten aus dem Alltag des Bergbaus verfügt es über ein Anschauungsbergwerk. Und wer sich für die Geschichte der Eisenbahn interessiert, wird im Süden der Stadt in Bochum-Dahlhausen fündig. Auf dem Gelände eines ehemaligen Bahnbetriebswerks sind historische Lokomotiven zu besichtigen. Das Haus Kemnade, ein Wasserschloss, verfügt unter anderem über eine Sammlung von historischen Musikinstrumenten. Ein Kuriosum: Das Schloss befindet sich eigentlich auf Hattinger Gebiet, gehört aber der Stadt Bochum. Das kulturelle Leben der Stadt verteilt sich auf über 20 Spielstätten. Das Schauspielhaus genießt dabei einen überregionalen Ruf. Und nach dem letzten Vorhang, wenn die Theater schließen, trifft man sich im Bermudadreieck, einer Ausgehmeile mit vielen Gaststätten und Szenelokalen um den Engelbertbrunnen, ganz in der Nähe des Schauspielhauses. Die Nachtschwärmer können sich dann mit einer Currywurst begnügen oder aber in eines der Szenelokale abtauchen – der Name des Viertels ist Programm.

Bochum is a town of museums. Among the twelve museums within its boundaries, the "German Mining Museum" (DBM) deserves a special mention as the center of research into the history of the coal and steel industry. You cannot miss the winding tower of the former "Germania" colliery, which was dismantled in 1974 in Dortmund and rebuilt in Bochum, and which has since become one of the town's main landmarks. The museum is the largest of its kind in the world. Apart from numerous exhibits portraying everyday life in the mining industry, it also boasts an exhibition mine. Those who are interested in the history of railroads will find what they are looking for in the south of the town, in Bochum-Dahlhausen. On the site of a former railway depot, you can inspect historic locomotives. Haus Kemnade is a moated castle which houses a collection of musical instruments. A curious fact is that the castle itself lies within the urban district of Hattingen, but actually belongs to Bochum. Within the town, cultural life is distributed across more than 20 locations. The theatre has a national reputation. After the last curtain call, the locals meet in the Bermudadreieck (Bermuda Triangle), an entertainment district with numerous restaurants and trendy bars around the Engelbert fountain, not far from the Schauspielhaus. Night owls enjoy a Currywurst (curry sausage) or disappear into one of the bars – as the name of the district indicates, it is the perfect place to get lost.

Von links oben im Uhrzeigersinn: Das Wasserschloss Haus Kemnade befindet sich eigentlich auf Hattinger Gebiet, gehört aber der Stadt Bochum; Eingangsbereich des Bergbaumuseums mit dem Förderturm „Germania"; Dampflok im Eisenbahnmuseum.

From top left clockwise: Haus Kemnade is a moated castle which actually lies within the urban district of Hattingen, but belongs to the Town of Bochum; Mining Museum, entrance with the "Germania" winding tower; steam locomotive in the Railroad Museum.

„Bochum, ich komm aus dir / Bochum, ich häng an dir / Glück auf, Bochum.“ *Herbert Grönemeyer, Sänger und Schauspieler*

“Bochum, I come from you / Bochum, I love you / Three cheers, Bochum.” *Herbert Grönemeyer, singer and actor*

Refugium
31
Wein
geöffnet
TEE & WEIN STUBE
AUCH VERKAUF
DARJEELINGS
FRÜCHTE TEE
Tee
Café

Hattingen, Ruhr-Aue und schönes Fachwerk

Hattingen, the Ruhr meadows and timbered buildings

Links: Ein Straßencafé am Kirchplatz in Hattingen. Oben: Das „Bügeleisenhaus" aus dem 17. Jahrhundert beherbergt das Museum des Heimatvereins.

Left: A pavement café on the church square in Hattingen. Above: The "Bügeleisenhaus" (17th century) houses the museum of the local history association.

Eine weitgehend intakte Altstadt mit etwa 150 mittelalterlichen Fachwerkhäusern macht die erstmals 990 schriftlich erwähnte Mittelstadt Hattingen zu einem beliebten Ausflugsziel. Besonders bemerkenswert ist das wegen seiner Form sogenannte Bügeleisenhaus und die St.-Georgs-Kirche mit ihrem schiefen Spitzhelm, der so geneigt gebaut wurde, damit er bei Sturm oder Blitzschlag nicht in das Kirchenschiff fiel. Die Grünflächen des Ruhrtals bei Hattingen ziehen im Sommer viele Erholungssuchende an. Hauptarbeitgeber war bis 1987 die Henrichshütte, eine der größten Eisen- und Stahlhütten der Region, heute Teil des Westfälischen Industriemuseums.

With its virtually intact Old Town including some 150 medieval timbered buildings, the medium-sized town of Hattingen – first mentioned in records in 990 – is a popular destination for excursions. Of particular interest are the "Bügeleisenhaus" (Iron House), so called because of its shape, and St. George's Church with its crooked spire, which was built in this way so that it would not fall onto the nave if it were damaged by a storm or struck by lightning. In summer, the green areas of the Ruhr valley near Hattingen attract many visitors in search of recreation. Until 1987, the main employer was the Henrichshütte, one of the biggest iron and steelworks in the region. Today, it is an industrial museum.

Witten, Herdecke und das Freilichtmuseum *Hagen*

Witten, Herdecke and Hagen open-air museum

Witten ist die größte Stadt im Ennepe-Ruhrkreis. Als eine der Stationen auf der Route der Industriekultur befindet sich im Stadtteil Bommern die Zeche Nachtigall. Bereits zu Beginn des 18. Jahrhunderts erhielten zwei Bauern die Erlaubnis, hier Kohle zu fördern. Auch der Name „Nachtigall“ stammt aus dieser Zeit. Das ehemalige Steinkohlebergwerk ist heute Teil des Westfälischen Industriemuseums, in dem unter anderem eine der ältesten Dampffördermaschinen besichtigt werden kann. Die kleine Stadt Herdecke liegt bei zwei Ruhrstauseen und ist deshalb ein beliebtes Naherholungsziel. Das imposante Ruhrviadukt, eine 30 Meter hohe und 313 Meter lange Eisenbahnbrücke, die 1879 eingeweiht wurde und nach ihrer Zerstörung bis 1957 wieder aufgebaut wurde, ist eines der Wahrzeichen der Stadt. Südlich von Herdecke liegt die kreisfreie Großstadt Hagen, die überregional besonders durch das Freilichtmuseum Hagen bekannt geworden ist. Während sich andere Freilichtmuseen typischerweise der bäuerlichen Kultur vergangener Zeiten widmen, thematisiert das unter der Trägerschaft des Landschaftsverbands Westfalen-Lippe 1960 gegründete Museum die Bereiche Handwerk und Technik. Etwa 60 Werkstätten sind auf dem 42 Hektar großen Gelände rekonstruiert und bieten Einblicke in die Entwicklung des Handwerks und der Technik vom ausgehenden 18. Jahrhundert bis hinein ins frühe 20. Jahrhundert.

Witten is the biggest town in the Ennepe-Ruhrkreis district. One of the main anchor points along the Industrial Heritage Trail is the Nachtigall (Nightingale) colliery in the Bommern district of town. At the beginning of the 18th century, two farmers were granted permission to start mining coal here. The name “Nachtigall” dates from this period. The former mineral coal mine is a museum today, in which you can see one of the oldest steam hauling engines alongside other exhibits. The little town of Herdecke lies beside two Ruhr reservoirs, which make it a popular recreational area. The imposing Ruhr viaduct is a railroad bridge which is 30 metres (98 feet) high and 313 metres (1027 feet) long and which was inuagurated in 1879. It was destroyed but then rebuilt in 1957; today it is one of the town’s main landmarks. South of Herdecke lies Hagen, a large town which is independent of the surrounding district and which is nationally famous for the Freilichtmuseum Hagen (Hagen open-air museum). While other open-air museums are typically dedicated to the farming culture of the past, this particular museum, founded in 1960 under the patronage of the countryside association of Westfalen-Lippe, focuses on the fields of crafts and technology. Some 60 workshops have been reconstructed on the 42-hectare (104-acre) site and offer a glimpse of the development of crafts and technology from the end of the 18th until the early 20th century.

Von oben links im Uhrzeigersinn: Herdecke, Eisenbahnviadukt; Zeche Nachtigall in Witten; Hagen Freilichtmuseum; Maschinenhalle der Zeche Nachtigall.

Clockwise from the top left: Herdecke, railroad viaduct; Nachtigall colliery in Witten; Hagen open-air museum; machinery hall of Nachtigall colliery;

Hagen – ein Kunstmäzen und der Jugendstil

Hagen – a patron of the arts and Art Nouveau

Über viele Jahrhunderte stand die heute kreisfreie, im Südosten des Ruhrgebiets gelegene Großstadt Hagen eher im Schatten ihrer Nachbarn. Erst im 18. Jahrhundert erlangte sie durch mehrere mit Wasserkraft betriebene Schmieden und Hammerwerke wirtschaftliche Bedeutung. Stadtrechte wurden dem Ort 1746 zugesprochen. Den Status einer Großstadt erreichte Hagen 1928 – die Schwerindustrie brachte vielen Menschen Arbeit. Dem Strukturwandel durch die Stahlkrise konnte sich auch Hagen nicht entziehen. Werke schlossen, die Region deindustrialisierte. Bei einigen Stahlsorten ist Hagen aber heute noch einer der europaweit führenden Standorte. Das Freilichtmuseum ist die überregional bekannteste Attraktion. Ein architektonisch bedeutendes Ensemble lohnt einen Abstecher in den Vorort Hagen-Ernst: der zwischen 1906 und 1908 nach Entwürfen des Jugendstilarchitekten Henry van de Velde (1863–1957) erbaute Hohenhof. Bauherr war der in Hagen geborene Kunstmäzen Karl Ernst Osthaus (1874–1921), der zu Beginn des 20. Jahrhunderts Leben und Kunst in einen neuen Einklang bringen wollte, Osthaus nannte dies den „Folkwang-Gedanken". Der Kunstmäzen initiierte unter anderem ein Museum der Weltkulturen. Hohenhof gehört heute der Stadt und beherbergt ein Kunstmuseum. Die Jugendstilinneneinrichtung von Henry van de Velde wurde aufwändig restauriert. Der Hohenhof ist einer der Ankerpunkte der Route der Industriekultur.

For many centuries, the city of Hagen in the southeast of the Ruhr region, and today a town independent of its neighboring district, was rather overshadowed by its neighbors. It was only in the 18th century that it achieved a degree of economic importance, thanks to a number of hydraulically powered forges and hammer mills. The town was awarded its municipal charter in 1746. It achieved city status in 1928 – heavy industry provided plenty of jobs. Like other places, Hagen was unable to escape the structural change brought about by the steel crisis. Factories closed and the region became de-industrialized. Nonetheless, for some types of steel Hagen remains one of the leading locations in Europe. Beyond the regional boundaries, the open-air museum is the best-known attraction. In the suburb of Hagen-Ernst there is an important architectural complex which is worth a detour: the Hohenhof was built here between 1906 and 1908 according to a design by the Art Nouveau architect Henry van de Velde (1863–1957). The client was Karl Ernst Osthaus (1874–1921), a patron of the arts, whose aim at the beginning of the 20th century was to strike a new balance between life and art. Among other projects, Osthaus initiated a Museum of World Cultures. Today, Hohenhof is owned by the municipality and houses an art museum. The Art Nouveau interior design has been meticulously restored. The Hohenhof is one of the anchor points along the Industrial Heritage Trail.

Der Hohenhof, Künstlerkolonie und Wohnhaus, wurde zwischen 1906 und 1908 nach Entwürfen des belgischen Jugendstilarchitekten Henry van de Velde erbaut. Bauherr war der Kunstmäzen Karl Ernst Osthaus. Heute beherbergt der Hohenhof ein Museum.

The Hohenhof, an artists' colony and residence, was built between 1906 and 1908 according to plans by the Belgian Art Nouveau architect Henry van de Velde. His client was Karl Ernst Osthaus, a patron of the arts. Today the Hohenhof houses a museum.

„Eiszeit, mit mir beginnt die Eiszeit, im Labyrinth der Eiszeit, minus 90 Grad."
Annette Humpe, in Hagen geborene Sängerin der Band „Ideal"

"Ice Age, the Ice Age begins with me, in the labyrinth of the Ice Age, minus 90 degrees." *Annette Humpe, singer of the band "Ideal", born in Hagen.*

SPECIAL | Theater und Kunst im Ruhrgebiet

Theatre and art in the Ruhr

Theater in der Gießerei

Die 1908 erbauten Flottmann-Hallen in Herne sind typisch für das, was den besonderen Charme der Theaterlandschaft des Ruhrgebiets ausmacht: Einst wurden dort Druckluftbohrhämmer für den Bergbau gefertigt, seit 1986 sind die Gebäude für Kabarett, Theater und Musical reserviert. Viele ehemalige Fabriken werden ähnlich genutzt. Das Ruhrgebiet verfügt über zahlreiche bedeutende Spielstätten, von den Mehrspartenhäusern in Essen, Dortmund, Duisburg, zu der Schauspielbühne Bochums, überregional bekannt durch mutige, oft provokative Inszenierungen, bis hin zu dem Starlight-Express-Theater in Bochum, in dem Andrew Lloyd Webbers aufwändig inszeniertes, gleichnamiges Eisenbahn-Musical seit über 20 Jahren die Zuschauer fasziniert. Die Ruhrfestspiele in Recklinghausen sind typisch für das kulturelle Selbstverständnis: Unter dem Leitgedanken, neue Kunstformen und andere Kulturen vorzustellen, treten hier namhafte Ensembles aus ganz Europa auf. Regionale Themen und Charaktere kommen im Mondpalast von Wanne-Eickel auf die Bühne, dem 2004 eröffneten ersten Volkstheater der Region.

Theatre in the foundry

Built in 1908, the Flottmann-Hallen in Herne are a typical example of the special charm of the theatre scene throughout the Ruhr region: In former times pneumatic drills were made here for the mining industry, but since 1986 the buildings have provided the stage for cabaret, plays and musicals. Many former factories are used for similar purposes. The Ruhr has a large number of important theatres, from the multi-use buildings in Essen, Dortmund and Duisburg to the stage in Bochum, nationally famous for its bold, often provocative productions, and the Starlight-Express Theatre in Bochum, in which Andrew Lloyd Webber's elaborately staged railway musical of the same name has been riveting audiences for more than 20 years. The Ruhr Festival in Recklinghausen is another typical examples of the Ruhrgebiet spririt: famous ensembles from all over Europe perform here with the aim of introducing new art forms and other cultures. The Ruhr itself and its local characters take the stage in the Mondpalast in Wanne-Eickel; the region's first folk theatre opened in 2004.

Piet-Mondrian-Plastik in Bottrop, Museum Quadrat; Plastik in Witten. Rechts: Museum Mülheim Alte Post.

Piet Mondrian sculpture in Bottrop, Museum Quadrat: sculpture in Witten. Right: Museum Alte Post, Mülheim.

Klare Farben und Linien

Die Kunst ist im Ruhrgebiet ohne Umwege in der Moderne angekommen. Klare Formen und Farben sowie technische Materialien herrschen vor – Piet Mondrian, die bemalten Eisenbahnschwellen auf der Halde Prosper Haniel, das Tetraeder in Bottrop. Brachliegende Industriegebäude werden auch hier neu genutzt: In den ehemaligen Schwarz- und Weißkauen der Zeche Unser Fritz 2/3 in Herne – den Räumen, in denen sich die Bergleute duschten und umzogen – arbeiten heute Künstler und Künstlerinnen. Das Museum Küppersmühle für moderne Kunst in Duisburg nutzt einen umgestalteten Getreidespeicher. Schwerpunkt ist die deutsche Malerei seit den 1950er-Jahren. Moderne Skulpturen sind im Museum Stiftung Wilhelm Lehmbruck in Duisburg zu sehen, Josef Albers Quadratstudien im Quadrat Bottrop, Lichtinstallationen im Zentrum für Lichtkunst in Unna. Kunstwerke zwischen „Blauer Reiter“, Fluxus und ZERO präsentiert das Dortmunder Museum am Ostwall. Der sympathische Name „Unperfekthaus“ bezeichnet ein Künstlerdorf mit Kneipe und Hotel in Essen. Kunst ist im Revier zu Hause.

Clear colors and lines

Art in the Ruhr has arrived straight in the modern age. Clear shapes and colors and high-tech materials predominate: a Piet Mondrian sculpture seems in place here, as do the painted railroad sleepers on the Prosper Haniel slag heap and the Tetraeder in Bottrop. Abandoned industrial buildings acquire a new lease on life: Today, artists have their studios in the “black and white” rooms of the “Unser Fritz 2/3” colliery in Herne – the former changing rooms in which the miners showered and changed their clothes. The Museum Küppersmühle, a modern art museum in Duisburg, is located in a converted grain store. It focuses on German painting since the 1950s. Modern sculpture can be viewed in the Stiftung Wilhelm Lehmbruck Museum in Duisburg, Josef Albers' square studies in the Quadrat Bottrop, light installations in the Zentrum für Lichtkunst in Unna. The Museum am Ostwall in Duisburg exhibits artworks from Der Blaue Reiter to Fluxus and ZERO. The endearing name “Unperfekthaus” (“Imperfect House”) refers to an artists' village with bar and hotel in Essen. The Ruhr has more than its fair share of art.

Links: Ruhrfestspielhaus Gelsenkirchen; Balletinszenierung, Essen. Rechts: Bottrop, Halde Prosper Haniel, Totems – bemalte Eisenbahnschwellen – von Ibarrola.

Left: Ruhrfestspielhaus in Gelsenkirchen; Ballet production in Essen. Right: Prosper Haniel slag heap in Bottrop: Totems – painted railroad sleepers – by Ibarrola.

Niederrhein und Lippe – von Duisburg bis Hamm

The Lower Rhine and Lippe – from Duisburg to Hamm

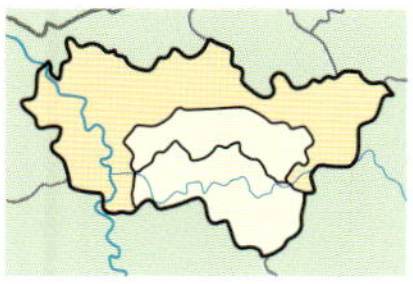

Die Städte in den westlichen und nördlichen Randgebieten um die Kernregion des Ruhrgebiets sind zwar Mitglieder im Regionalverband Ruhr, betonen aber zugleich ihre Eigenständigkeit. Die niederrheinische Großstadt Duisburg, als größter Binnenhafen, ist untrennbar mit den weiter östlich gelegenen Industriezentren verbunden. Bisweilen gehen die Grenzen mitten durch die Städte. In Teilen von Hamm, Lünen und Haltern fühlen sich die Einwohner bereits als Münsterländer.

The towns on the western and northern borders of the main Ruhr region still belong to the Ruhr regional association, but like to emphasize their independence. The Lower Rhine city of Duisburg, the largest inland port, is inseparably linked to the industrial centres further to the east. In some cases, the boundaries even pass through the towns themselves. In some parts of Hamm and Lünen and in Haltern am See the inhabitants feel a closer kinship with the Münsterland.

Duisburg – das „stählerne Herz Europas“ …

Duisburg – the “steel heart of Europe”…

Am Westrand des Ruhrgebiets am Übergang zum Niederrhein liegt die kreisfreie Großstadt Duisburg, für viele Deutsche bekannt geworden über den von Götz George verkörperten Tatort-Kommissar Horst Schimanski. Duisburg liegt an der Mündung der Ruhr in den Rhein, im Norden der Stadtgebiets entwässert die Alte Emscher in den Rhein. Dank der verkehrsgünstigen Lage verfügt die Stadt über den größten Binnenhafen der Welt. Große Traditionsunternehmen sind hier ansässig, darunter die Klöckner-Werke, ThyssenKrupp und Mannesmann. Für die Alliierten gehörte Duisburg mit seinen Industrieanlagen und dem Hafen zu den strategisch wichtigen Zielen, im Bombenhagel wurde die Altstadt und der Hafen zu fast 90 Prozent zerstört. Nach dem Krieg erwies sich die Schwerindustrie erst einmal als Motor des Aufstiegs, doch die Stahl- und Kohlekrise erfasste auch Duisburg. Die Stadt ist jedoch bis heute ein Zentrum der Stahlindustrie geblieben: Alle sieben der im Ruhrgebiet noch aktiven Hochöfen befinden sich hier. Zugleich entwickelte sich die Stadt zu einem Zentrum für unternehmensnahe Dienstleistungen. Das nach dem in Duisburg geborenen Bildhauer Wilhelm Lehmbruck (1881–1919) benannte Museum ist eine der Hauptattraktionen der Stadt. Es beherbergt neben zahlreichen Plastiken des Künstlers und anderer Bildhauer des 20. Jahrhunderts auch eine umfangreiche Sammlung deutscher Malerei des späten 19. und 20. Jahrhunderts.

The city of Duisburg lies on the western borders of the Ruhr region, where the latter gives way to the Lower Rhine. Duisburg is famous throughout Germany as the home of Inspector Horst Schimanski, played by Götz George and a protagonist of the television detective series “Tatort”. Duisburg lies where the Ruhr flows into the Rhine; in the northern part of the built-up area the Alter Emscher also flows into the Rhine. Thanks to its favorable location, the city can boast the largest river port in the world. A number of important firms are here, including the Klöckner-Werke, ThyssenKrupp and Mannesmann. During the Third Reich, Duisburg was a center of the armaments industry. For the Allies, the town, its industrial plants and port were one of the main targets, so that almost 90 percent of the Old Town and the port were destroyed during the bombing raids. After the war, heavy industry served as a motor for economic progress in the first instance, but the coal and steel crisis hit Duisburg, too. However, Duisburg remains to this day one of the main centres of the steel industry: All seven of the blast furnaces in operation in the Ruhr region will be found here. At the same time, the city has developed into a center for business services. One of the main attractions is the museum, named after Wilhelm Lehmbruck (1881–1919), the sculptor born in Duisburg. Apart from Lehmbruck’s works, many paintings of German artists from the end of the 19th and the 20th century are on display.

Seite 68, 69 von links im Uhrzeigersinn: Duisburger Hafen, am Zusammenfluss von Rhein und Ruhr; Eselsskulptur in Wesel; Moers, Halde Rheinpreußen mit Geleucht von Otto Piene, rechts in Form einer riesigen Grubenlampe; Schafherde bei Wesel; Xanten, Fenster am Klever Tor.

Pages 68, 69 clockwise from the left: Duisburg port at the confluence of the Rhine and the Ruhr; the donkey sculpture in Wesel; Moers, the Rheinpreußen slagheap with illumination by Otto Piene on the right, in the form of an enormous miner’s lamp; herd of sheep near Wesel; Xanten, a window of the Klever Tor.

Von links oben im Uhrzeigersinn: Dreigiebelhaus; Innenraum der Ditip-Merkez-Moschee; Rathaus und Stadttheater.

Clockwise from top left: Dreigiebelhaus (Three-gabled house); interior of the Ditip-Merkez mosque; town hall and municipal theatre.

... mit dem größten *Binnenhafen* der Welt

... with the largest river port in the world

Winter im Duisburger Landschaftspark Nord, stillgelegtes Stahlwerk; Raddampfer „Oscar Huber“; Kontor im Haniel-Museum; Schwanentorbrücke.

Winter in the countryside park Nord in Duisburg, decommissioned steelworks; the paddle steamer “Oscar Huber”; office in the Haniel Museum; Schwanentor Bridge.

Der Duisburg-Ruhrort-Hafen, der ein Areal von etwa zehn Quadratkilometern einnimmt, ist durch die Anbindung an die großen Seehäfen Amsterdam, Rotterdam und Hamburg zu einem Umschlagplatz für Waren aller Art geworden. Der Binnenschifffahrt ist im Stadtteil Ruhrort ein Museum gewidmet, zu dem auch der Raddampfer „Oscar Huber“ gehört. Das älteste Gebäude Ruhrorts beherbergt das kleine Haniel-Museum. Dort wird unter anderem gezeigt, wie ein Büro – ein Kontor – im 19. Jahrhundert ausgesehen hat. Damals führte man noch handschriftlich Buch, und die Pegelstände wichtiger Orte notierte man auf einer Schiefertafel.

The river port of Duisburg-Ruhrort, which covers an area of about ten square kilometres (3.86 square miles), has become a trans-shipment point for goods of every description, thanks to its links with the great seaports of Amsterdam, Rotterdam and Hamburg. A museum in the district of Ruhrort has been dedicated to the subject of inland shipping; one of the exhibits is the paddle steamer “Oscar Huber”. The oldest building in Ruhrort houses the little Haniel Museum. There you can see, for example, what an office looked like during the 19th century. In those days bookkeeping was carried out by hand, and the water levels at important places were noted on a blackboard.

Römer- und Siegfriedstadt *Xanten*

Xanten – Roman town and birthplace of Siegfried

Für Puristen gehört Xanten nicht mehr zum Ruhrgebiet im engeren Sinne, sondern zum Niederrhein. Wer immer aber das Ruhrgebiet besucht, wird auf dem westlichen Auge nicht blind sein – auch die offiziellen Tourismusagenturen und Führer berücksichtigen stets die Römerstadt. Und das aus gutem Grund: Xanten blickt auf eine über 2000-jährige Geschichte zurück. Die Römer errichteten 13/12 v. Chr. ein erstes Lager in der Nähe der heutigen Stadt; 110 n. Chr. gründeten sie dort die Colonia Ulpia Traiana, mit etwa 10000 Einwohnern die drittgrößte Römerstadt nördlich der Alpen. An die Römerzeit wird im Archäologischen Park erinnert, einem großen Freilichtmuseum, das sich teilweise auf dem Gelände der früheren Colonia befindet. Auch in den Sagen des Mittelalters spielt der Ort eine große Rolle: Xanten gilt als der Geburtsort Siegfrieds, des Drachentöters der Nibelungensage. Die Stadt bildet den Anfang der Nibelungenroute, einer Wander- und Radwanderroute zu den Schauplätzen der Sage. Sehenswert ist in Xanten darüber hinaus der imposante mittelalterliche Dom St. Viktor, dessen Grundstein 1263 gelegt wurde. Erst 1544 kam der Kirchenbau zum Abschluss. Er ist dem heiligen Viktor geweiht, einem Märtyrer aus dem 4. Jahrhundert n. Chr. Als Teil der mittelalterlichen Stadtbefestigung ist das 1393 erbaute Klever Doppeltor erhalten. Das innere Tor verfügt über Ferienapartments.

Purists are of the opinion that Xanten no longer really belongs to the Ruhr region proper, but rather to the Lower Rhine. Visitors to the Ruhr, however, will not turn a blind eye to the west as a whole – even official tourist offices and guidebooks always include the Roman town. With good reason: Xanten's history stretches back over 2,000 years. In 13/12 B.C. the Romans built their first camp near today's town; In 110 A.D. they founded the Colonia Ulpia Traiana there; with a population of about 10,000 inhabitants it was the third-largest Roman town north of the Alps. Today the Archeological Park, a vast open-air museum, recalls the Roman era. Part of it even lies on the site of the former Colonia. The place was also important in the sagas of medieval times: Xanten is said to be the birthplace of Siegfried, the dragon-slayer in the saga of the Nibelungs. Xanten marks the start of the Nibelung Trail, a cycling and hiking route to the scenes of the legend. In Xanten the impressive medieval St Viktor's cathedral is also worth seeing; its foundation stone was laid in 1263. The church was not completed until 1544. It is dedicated to St Viktor, a martyr who lived during the 4th century A.D. Also intact is the Klever Doppeltor, built in 1393 as part of the town's medieval fortifications. The inner section of the gateway houses holiday apartments.

Von links im Uhrzeigersinn: Diese gewaltige, teilrekonstruierte römische Tempelanlage im Ärchäologischen Park Xanten wurde auf einem drei Meter hohen Podium errichtet; das Klever Tor ist ein Doppeltor und es gehörte zur mittelalterlichen Stadtbefestigung, im Bild ist das innere Tor zu sehen; die Westfassade des gotischen Doms St. Viktor.

Clockwise from the left: The partly reconstructured Roman temple in the Xanten archeological park is placed on a platform which is three metres (nine feet) tall; the Klever Gate is a double gate, the picture shows the inner gate; the western façade of St Viktor's Cathedral.

Wesel, Festungsstadt an der Lippemündung

Wesel, the fortified town at the mouth of the Lippe

Links: Das 1718 errichtete Haupttor der Zitadelle Wesel, der einstige Kern der Festung Wesel. Oben: Der evangelische Willibrordi-Dom ist innen lichtdurchflutet.

Left: The main gate of the citadel of Wesel was erected in 1718. Above: The interior of the Protestant St Willibrord's Cathedral is flooded with light.

Jedes Echo weiß, wie der Bürgermeister von Wesel heißt, wenn es von den Bergen „Esel, Esel…“ zurückschallt – der Kalauer ist jedem Kind geläufig. Selbstbewusst und spielerisch nutzt die Hansestadt am nordwestlichen Rand des Ruhrgebiets das Motiv: Mehrere bunte „Esel-von-Wesel“-Skulpturen schmücken das Stadtbild. Die evangelische Stadtkirche, der spätgotische Willibrordi-Dom, ist dem angelsächsischen Missionar Willibrord (um 658 – 739), dem Gründer des Klosters Echternach, gewidmet. Die im 17./18. Jahrhundert erbaute Zitadelle ist die größte Festungsanlage des Rheinlands. Heute beherbergt sie unter anderem zwei Museen und das Stadtarchiv.

Local children all know the nonsense rhyme to the effect that every echo repeats the name of the mayor of Wesel, when the surrounding hills resound to the sound of "Esel, Esel…" (Donkey, donkey…) The Hanseatic City on the northwestern edge of the Ruhr region uses the motif in a self-confident, playful manner. A number of brightly colored "Esel von Wesel" (Wesel donkey) statues adorn the town. The Protestant parish church, the late Gothic St. Willibrord's Cathedral, is dedicated to the Anglo-Saxon missionary Willibrord (c. 658 – 739), the founder of Echternach Monastery. The citadel (17th/18th century) is the largest fortified complex in the Rhineland. Today, it houses two museums and the town archives.

Dinslaken – Stadt im grünen Gürtel

Dinslaken – a town within the green belt

Im Nordwesten des Ruhrgebiets wenige Kilometer südöstlich von Wesel liegt die Hansestadt Dinslaken, der Namenbestandteil „laken" verweist auf die vielen Tümpel, die es einst in der Stadt gab. Erstmals urkundlich erwähnt wurde Dinslaken im 12. Jahrhundert, Marktrechte erhielt der Ort 1478, und 1540 erfolgte der Beitritt zur Hanse. Zwischen 1906 und 1912 wurde die Zeche Lohberg errichtet, in der 1909 zum ersten Mal Kohle gefördert wurde; erst Ende 2005 wurde die Zeche geschlossen. Ein Ereignis wird in der Stadt in trauriger Erinnerung gehalten: In der Reichspogromnacht 1938 wurden nicht nur die Geschäfte und Wohnhäuser jüdischer Bürger, die Synagoge sowie das jüdische Waisenhaus zerstört, sondern auch 35 Waisenkinder und ein Lehrer aus der Stadt vertrieben – über deren weiteres Schicksal ist nichts bekannt. Eine Skulptur des Dinslakener Künstlers Alfred Grimm in der Nähe des Rathauses erinnert an diesen sogenannten Judenzug. Zu den unbelasteten Erinnerungsstücken, die in der Stadt gepflegt werden, zählt eine alte Wassermühle von 1693 im Stadtteil Hiesfeld. Dank der Initiative eines Vereins ist sie restauriert und an Sonntagen als Mühlenmuseum zugänglich. Anhand vieler Modelle aus aller Welt wird die Arbeitsweise der unterschiedlichen Typen von Mühlen erklärt. Ebenfalls restauriert und als Museum zugänglich ist die alte Turmwindmühle, eines der Wahrzeichen von Dinslaken.

The Hanseatic town of Dinslaken lies in the northwest of the Ruhr region, a few kilometres southeast of Wesel. The expression "laken" which forms part of the name is a reference to the numerous ponds which were once scattered across the town. The first records of Dinslaken crop up in the 12th century; the town was granted market rights in 1478, and it joined the Hanseatic League in 1540. Lohberg colliery was founded between 1906 and 1912; coal was first mined here in 1909; the mine was not closed until the end of 2005. One event which the town remembers with great sadness was the Night of Broken Glass in 1938, when not only the shops and homes of Jewish citizens, the synagogue and the Jewish orphanage were destroyed; 35 orphans and a teacher were driven out of town – no one knows what happened to them. A sculpture by the local artist Alfred Grimm near the Town Hall recalls this event, known as the Judenzug. Among the souvenirs without such problematic memories which the town retains are an old water mill dating from 1693 in the Hiesfeld district of town. It has been restored on the initiative of an association; the Mühlenmuseum (Mill Museum) is open to the public on Sundays. The way mills work is explained using examples from all over the world. Also restored and accessible as a museum is the old tower windmill which is one of Dinslaken's main landmarks.

Das Mühlenmuseum im Stadtteil Hiesfeld liegt zu beiden Seiten des Rotbachs. Das Fachwerkhaus wurde nach dem Muster der ursprünglichen Wassermühle von 1693 wieder hergestellt; der Backsteinbau auf der anderen Seite des Bachs ist späteren Datums und war das Hauptgebäude des Mühlenbetriebs und Wohnhaus des Müllers.

The Mill museum in the Hiesfeld district of town lies on both banks of the Rotbach. The timbered house was restored according to the design of the original water mill dating from 1693; the brick building on the other side of the stream is of a later date and was the main building of the mill operations and the miller's residence.

„Gott setzte mich in Dinslaken ab und fragte mich: Samma, willze en Heiligenschein?“ Hanns Dieter Hüsch (1925–2005), Kabarettist

“God put me down in Dinslaken and asked me: Tell me, do you want a halo?” Hanns Dieter Hüsch (1925–2005), cabaret artist

Moers, alte Grafenstadt am Niederrhein

Moers, the ancient aristocratic town on the Lower Rhine

Die ehemalige Bergarbeitersiedlung Meerbeck, die zwischen 1907 und 1913 in unmittelbarer Nachbarschaft der Zeche Rheinpreußen erbaut wurde.

Meerbeck former miners' settlement, which was built between 1907 and 1913 in the immediate vicinity of Rheinpreußen colliery.

Erstmals urkundlich erwähnt wurde Moers als „Murse" im 9. Jahrhundert in den Heberegistern des Klosters Werden. Im Juli 1300 erhielt Moers die Stadtrechte, 1373 folgte das Münzrecht. Ab 1597 stand die Stadt unter niederländischer Herrschaft, wurde zu einer Festung ausgebaut und erlebte eine Blütezeit. 1702 kam Moers im Wege der Erbfolge an Preußen, wurde 1706 Fürstentum und damit reichsunmittelbar. Ab 1798 geriet die Stadt unter französische Herrschaft als Teil der von den Franzosen eroberten linksrheinischen Territorien. Nach der Niederlage Napoleons wurden die niederrheinischen Gebiete – und damit auch Moers – 1815 auf dem Wiener Kongress wieder Preußen zugeschlagen. Der Bergbau begann gegen Ende des 19. Jahrhunderts. Zwischen 1900 und 1904 wurde die Schachtanlage Rheinpreußen 4 niedergebracht; sie war zwar eine Anschlussanlage der Duisburger Zeche gleichen Namens des Unternehmers Franz Haniel, arbeitete allerdings eigenständig. Zeitgleich wurde unmittelbar daneben mit dem Bau einer Siedlung für 10000 Menschen begonnen: die Bergarbeitersiedlung Meerbeck. Der im Zweiten Weltkrieg weitgehend zerstörte Stadtteil wurde 1980 in Teilen wieder rekonstruiert.

Moers was first mentioned in records in the 9th century as "Murse" in the property register of Werden monastery. Moers was granted municipal rights in July 1300, and in 1373 there followed the right to mint coins. Beginning in 1597, the town was under Dutch rule; it was transformed into a fortress and enjoyed a golden age. In 1702, Moers was ceded to Prussia; in 1706, it became a principality and thus enjoyed Imperial immediacy. In 1798, the town came under French rule as part of the territories on the left bank of the Rhine. After Napoleon's defeat, the Lower Rhine territories, including Moers, were ceded to Prussia again in 1815 during the Congress of Vienna. Mining began here at the end of the 19th century. Between 1900 and 1904, the shaft complex Rheinpreußen 4 was constructed; it was designed to connect with the Duisburg colliery of the same name owned by the industrialist Franz Haniel, although it operated independently. At the same time, construction of an estate for 10,000 people had begun: the Meerbeck miners' settlement. This district of town was largely destroyed in World War II but some sections were rebuilt in 1980.

Schacht 4 war bis 1962 in Betrieb. Nach Stilllegung und Verfüllung wurde er 1988 umfassend saniert. Inzwischen gilt die Anlage als Industriedenkmal und ist Teil der Route der Industriekultur. Doch in Moers lässt sich auch auf den Spuren der älteren Geschichte wandeln: Das Schloss, Wahrzeichen von Moers, befindet sich mitten im Zentrum und gilt als das älteste Gebäude der Stadt. In der Zeit der niederländischen Herrschaft Anfang des 17. Jahrhunderts wurde es mit fünf Bastionen verstärkt, auch die Stadt Moers selbst erhielt eine Befestigung. Die Wehranlagen wurden allerdings unter den Preußen geschleift. Das Schloss wurde in Teilen abgerissen und verfiel. 1905 erwarb die Stadt Moers das Gelände, 1938 wurde das Schlossgebäude hergerichtet und dient heute als Museum und Ort für kulturelle Veranstaltungen wie Theateraufführungen oder Konzerte. Das 1975 eröffnete Schlosstheater zählt zu den kleinsten Bühnen Deutschlands. Die Statue der Kurfürstin Louise Henriette von Oranien vor dem Schloss erinnert an die Zeit der niederländischen Herrschaft. Geschaffen hat sie 1909 der Düsseldorfer Bildhauer Heinrich Baucke.

Shaft 4 continued to operate until 1962. After it was decommissioned and filled in, it was meticulously renovated in 1988. Today the site is regarded as an industrial memorial and is an anchor point along the Industrial Heritage Trail. But in Moers you can also trace the development of the town's older history. The castle, Moers' principal landmark, lies in the center of town and is thought to be the oldest building in town. During the early 17th century, when the town was ruled by the Dutch, it was reinforced with five bulwarks. The town itself was also fortified. However, the fortifications were demolished under the Prussians. The castle was pulled down in sections and fell into ruin. In 1905, the town of Moers acquired the site and over thirty years later, the castle building was reconstructed. Today, it serves as a museum and a stage for cultural events such as plays of concerts. The castle houses one of the smallest theatres of Germany, which was opened in 1975. The statue of Electress Louise Henriette of Orange in front of the castle recalls the period of Dutch rule. It was created in 1909 by the Düsseldorf sculptor Heinrich Baucke.

Das Moerser Schloss mit dem 1909 geschaffenen Standbild der Kurfürstin Louise Henriette von Oranien (1627–1667).

Moers Castle with the statue of Electress Louise Henriette of Orange (1627–1667), created in 1909.

Dorsten – Mittelstadt mit Wasserschloss

Dorsten – a medium-sized town with a moated castle

Am nördlichen Rand des Ruhrgebiets im Übergangsbereich zum Münsterland liegt die Stadt Dorsten. Durch die Stadt fließt die Lippe und der Wesel-Datteln-Kanal, eine der verkehrsreichsten Wasserstraßen Deutschlands. Die erstmals 1251 urkundlich erwähnte Stadt gehört zum Kreis Recklinghausen. Auch hier spielte die Kohleförderung eine große Rolle, die Zechen Fürst Leopold und Baldur haben Anfang des letzten Jahrhunderts die Förderung aufgenommen (2001 wurde der Bergbau eingestellt). Im Dorstener Stadtteil Lembeck liegt das gleichnamige Schloss, ein Wasserschloss, dessen heutiges Aussehen auf barocke Um- und Ausbauten gegen Ende des 17. Jahrhunderts zurückgeht. Die Anlage ist in Privatbesitz, wird aber für vielfältige Zwecke verwendet. Sie beherbergt ein Heimatmuseum und ein Schlossmuseum, eine Galerie und eine Schlosskapelle, die auch gerne für Taufen oder Trauungen eingesetzt wird. Im Festsaal finden darüber hinaus regelmäßig Konzerte statt. Die Anlage des Parks erfolgte im Zuge der barocken Umbauarbeiten zunächst auch im barocken Stil nach französischem Vorbild. Im 19. Jahrhundert wurde der Park allerdings als englischer Landschaftsgarten umgestaltet und ist heute beliebtes Ausflugsziel. Blumenfreunde aus nah und fern tummeln sich besonders in der Zeit der Rhododendronblüte in den Monaten Juni und Juli im unmittelbar an den Park angrenzenden Heinrich-Nottelmann-Park.

The town of Dorsten lies on the northern edge of the Ruhr region, where it gives way to the Münsterland, where many people still make a living in agriculture. Both the Lippe and the Wesel-Datteln canal, one of the busiest waterways in Germany, flow through the town. The town, first mentioned in records in 1251, lies within the Recklinghausen district. Here, too, coal mining plays an important role; the Fürst Leopold and Baldur collieries began extracting coal at the beginning of the last century; mining here ended in 2001. Lembeck Castle lies in the district of town of the same name. It is a moated castle whose present appearance goes back to a Baroque rebuilding and extension at the end of the 17th century. The complex is privately owned but is used for a wide range of purposes. It houses a museum of local history and a castle museum, a gallery and the castle chapel which often provides the setting for baptisms and weddings. Concerts are also held regularly in the ballroom. During the Baroque rebuilding of the castle, the park was initially also laid out in Baroque style after the French model. However, during the 19th century it was redesigned as an English landscape garden and is a popular excursion destination today. Flower-lovers from near and far especially enjoy a visit when the rhododendrons are flowering in June and July in Heinrich Nottelmann Park, next door to the castle park.

Schloss Lembeck befindet sich bei Dorsten im Übergangsbereich vom nördlichen Ruhrgebiet zum Münsterland. Das Schloss wurde erstmals 1177 urkundlich erwähnt.

Lembeck Castle lies near Dorsten where the northern Ruhr region gives way to the Münsterland. The castle was first mentioned in records in 1177.

Trennkost-Seminar

Haltern am See und *Lünen* – am Übergang zum Münsterland

Haltern am See and Lünen – on the edge of the Münsterland

Links: Haltern, Rathaus. Oben: Das „Ufo" – der Lüntec-Tower im Technologiezentrum, ein umgestalteter Förderturm, mit dem „Colani-Ei", zu sehen in Lünen.

Left: Haltern, Town Hall. Above: The "Ufo" – the Lüntec Tower in the Technology Centre, a converted windingtower with the "Colani-Ei" (Colani Egg), Lünen.

Haltern am See im Grenzbereich von Ruhrgebiet und Münsterland kam über eine Kreisreform zum Kreis Recklinghausen. Hier fehlen die sonst für das Ruhrgebiet typischen Industrieansiedlungen. Die Mittelstadt liegt im Naturpark Hohe Mark, umgeben von Seen und eingebettet in Wald – ein beliebtes Naherholungsgebiet. Lünen im Kreis Unna, der zum Regionalverband Ruhrgebiet gehört, zeigt sowohl ländliche als auch industrielle Züge – hier trifft das Ruhrgebiet auf das Münsterland. Besonders kreativ wurde hier der ehemalige Förderturm der Steinkohlenzeche „Minister Achenbach" nach Plänen des Designers Colani umgestaltet – im Volksmund „Ufo" genannt.

Haltern am See lies on the border between the Ruhr region and the Münsterland. Following the local government boundary reform, it now forms part of the Recklinghausen district. You will not find here the industrial installations typical of the Ruhr region. It is a medium-sized town lying at the heart of the Hohe Mark Nature Park, surrounded by lakes and nestled in woodland – a popular recreational area. Lünen in the district of Unna demonstrates both rural and industrial aspects – here, too, the Ruhr region and the Münsterland meet. The former winding tower of the Minister Achenbach mineral coal mine was creatively re-designed by the designer Luigi Colani: It is known locally as the "Ufo".

Unna und *Hamm* – Esel und Glaselefant

Unna and Hamm – the donkey and the glass elephant

Der Esel gehört nicht nur zu Wesel, sondern auch zu Unna, der Kreisstadt des gleichnamigen Kreises im Osten des Ruhrgebiets. Hier ist es kein zufälliges Echo, vielmehr gibt es mehrere Geschichten, die den Esel mit Unna in Verbindung bringen. In einem Reisebericht aus dem 18. Jahrhundert bemerkt ein Pfarrer, dass die Einwohner viele Esel halten, was dem Ort den spöttischen Beinamen „Eselsakademie" eintrug. Zur 700-Jahr-Feier der Stadt 1950 marschierte ein Esel dem Festzug voran und seit 1978 schmückt ein Brunnen mit einer Eselskulptur aus Bronze den Marktplatz der Stadt. Der Esel wird durchaus positiv gesehen; er gilt als stur und ab und zu störrisch, zugleich aber als arbeitssam – und so sehen sich auch die Westfalen. Man munkelt, dass im Stadtrat auch einmal die Idee diskutiert wurde, die Brücke über den Stadtring „Eselsbrücke" zu nennen – doch der Vorschlag setzte sich nicht durch. Ganz in der Nähe von Unna liegt die kreisfreie Großstadt Hamm, die bereits 1226 als Planstadt gegründet wurde. Die Attraktion der Stadt ist sicherlich der Glaselefant im Maximilianpark, eine etwa 35 Meter hohe, begehbare Plastik, die der Künstler Horst Rellecke 1984 aus Anlass der Landesgartenschau um die ehemalige Kohlenwäsche der Zeche Maximilian errichtete. Im Glaselefanten sind zur Freude nicht nur der Kinder einige kinetische Objekte zu sehen, die auf Knopfdruck in Aktion gesetzt werden können.

The donkey does not only belong to Wesel, but also to Unna, the district town in the east of the Ruhr district. Here there is no random echo, but rather a number of stories, to explain the link between Unna and the donkey. In a travel journal dating from the 18th century, a priest noticed that the inhabitants kept a lot of donkeys, which resulted in the town being given the nickname of "Eselsakademie" (donkey academy). In 1950, to mark the town's 700th anniversary, a donkey led the procession. Since 1978, a fountain with a bronze sculpture of a donkey has adorned the town market place. The donkey is seen in a positive light: it is regarded as stubborn, sometimes even obstinate, but it is also hard-working – which is how the citizens of Westphalia also see themselves. People speculate that the town council even considered calling the bridge over the ring road "Eselsbrücke" (donkey's bridge) – but the proposal did not find sufficient support. Near Unna lies the city of Hamm, which is independent of its surrounding district and which was founded in 1226. The town's main attraction is the Glass Elephant in the Maximilianpark, a sculpture some 35 metres (115 feet) high. The artist Horst Rellecke had it erected in 1984 on the occasion of the state gardens exhibition around the former coal washery of the Maximilian colliery. Within the Glass Elephant not only children are amused by the kinetic objects on display, which can be put into action at the touch of a button.

Von Links: Unna, Nicolaiviertel, darunter der Eselsbrunnen von 1978; Rechts: Hamm, Maximilianpark mit dem, um die ehemalige Kohlenwäscherei der Zeche Maximilian gebauten Glaselefanten. Folgende Doppelseite: Wald im Naturpark Hohe Mark.

Left: Unna, Nicolai district, below donkey fountain (1978); Right: Hamm, the Glass Elephant in the Maximilianpark, erected around the former coal washery of the Maximilian colliery. Next double page: Forest in Hohe Mark Nature Park.

„Der freundliche Overweg in Unna, die angenehmen Tage in Hamm … alles steht noch lebendig vor mir.“
Heinrich Heine, 1822 in einem Brief, „Overweg“ meint ein Gasthaus in Unna

“The friendly Overweg in Unna, the pleasant days in Hamm … I still remember it all very clearly.”
Heinrich Heine, 1822 in a letter, “Overweg” refers to an inn in Unna

Die schönsten Touren zwischen Lippe und Ruhr

The most picturesque tours betwen the rivers Lippe and Ruhr

Vier Tourenvorschläge für Auto-, Radfahrer und Wanderer sind hier zusammengestellt. Meist handelt es sich um die im Ruhrgebiet liegenden Teilabschnitte längerer Routen.

Summarized below are four suggested routes for car drivers, cyclists and hikers. Most of them are sections of longer routes.

Die Route der Industriekultur/Industrial Heritage Trail

Dortmund – Lünen – Hamm – Unna – Hagen – Witten – Hattingen – Essen – Mülheim a.d. Ruhr – Duisburg – Oberhausen – Gelsenkirchen – Bochum – Recklinghausen – Waltrop – Dortmund, 400 km (250 miles)

Dieser Abschnitt der Route der Industriekultur verbindet die wichtigsten Industrie- und Kulturdenkmäler des Ruhrgebiets: Vom UNESCO-Weltkulturerbe Zeche Zollverein und der kruppschen Villa Hügel in Essen spannt sich der Bogen bis zum Maximilianpark in Hamm und zum Westfälischen Freilichtmuseum in Hagen, vom Schiffshebewerk Henrichenburg bis zum Duisburger Hafen, dem größten Binnenhafen Europas, und zum Gasometer beim Einkaufs- und Freizeitzentrum CentrO in Oberhausen. Zu den Höhepunkten der Route zählen ferner viele Aussichtspunkte.

This section of the Industrial Heritage Trail links the principal industrial and cultural monuments of the Ruhr region: It extends from the Zollverein coal mine, part of the UNESCO World Cultural Heritage, and the Krupp family's Villa Hügel in Essen to the Maximilianpark in Hamm and the Westphalian open-air museum in Hagen; from the Henrichenburg ship lift to the port of Duisburg, the largest river port In Europe; and on to the gasometer at the CentrO shopping and leisure center in Oberhausen.The highlights of the route also include a number of scenic viewpoints.

Info: www.route-industriekultur.de

Ruhrtal-Radweg

Hengsteysee – Baldeneysee – Duisburg, 60 km (37.5 miles)

Der RuhrtalRadweg folgt der Namengeberin des Ruhrgebiets von der Quelle bei Winterberg im Hochsauerland bis zur Mündung in den Niederrhein in Duisburg. Der hier vorgeschlagene Teilabschnitt verbindet die Wassersportseen Hengstey-, Harkort-, Kemnader und Baldeneysee. Die abwechslungsreiche Fahrt folgt vielfach den historischen Treidelpfaden längs des Flusses im Grünen, dazwischen liegen malerische Fachwerkorte wie Hattingen, das zwischen bewaldeten Hügeln eines der schönsten Altstadtbilder Westfalens bewahrt hat.

The Ruhr Valley cycle path follows the river which gave its name to the region from its source near Winterberg in the Upper Sauerland to the point where it flows into the Lower Rhine in Duisburg. The section suggested here links the Hengsteysee, Harkortsee, Kemnader See and Baldeneysee lakes, used for aquatic sports. The route is scenically varied and follows in many cases the historic towpaths along the river in a rural setting, passing picturesque villages of timbered houses such as Hattingen, which lies between wooded hills and has retained one of the most attractive historic town centers in Westphalia.

Info: www.ruhrtalradweg.com

Radroute Dortmund-Ems-Kanal

Dortmund – Henrichenburg – Dortmund, 32 km (20 miles)

Die Radroute Dortmund-Ems-Kanal folgt auf autofreien Kanaluferwegen dem 1899 eröffneten Kanal von Dortmund bis zum Seebad Norddeich. Auf verkehrsfreien Wegen im Grünen führt die Auftaktetappe vom Naherholungs- und Freizeitpark Fredenbaum in Dortmund zum Schleusenpark Waltrop, mit dem historischen Schiffshebewerk Henrichenburg an der Einmündung des Rhein-Herne-Kanals.

The Dortmund-Ems Canal cycle path follows traffic-free paths along the banks of the canal from Dortmund to to the sea resort of Norddeich. The first section leads along traffic-free paths through countryside, from Fredenbaum recreational and leisure park in Dortmund to Waltrop lock park by the historic Henrichenburg ship lift at the confluence with the Rhine-Herne Canal.

Info: www.routenplaner.nrw.de

Vier Genießertouren – mit dem Auto (rot), mit dem Fahrrad (grün) oder zu Fuß (violett).

Four of the most beautiful tours – by car (red), bicycle (green) or on foot (purple).

Ruhrhöhenweg

Dortmund-Hohensyburg – Hattingen – Essen-Steele, 60 km (37.5 miles), 2–3 Tage (2 – 3 days)

Der Ruhrhöhenweg ist die Topadresse für naturnahes Wandern im Ruhrgebiet. Anders als der Ruhrtal-Radweg führt er kaum durch das Tal selbst, sondern über die bewaldeten Hänge. Burgruinen wie die Hohensyburg, die Isenburg oder der Blankenstein bieten prachtvolle Ausblicke. Pfadartige Passagen durch Buchenwälder und bequeme Wirtschaftswege wechseln hier einander ab. Der vorgeschlagene Abschnitt lässt sich in zwei bis drei Tagen bewältigen. Das kuppige Gelände mit immer wieder steilen Auf- und Abstiegen erfordert ein wenig Kondition. Den Weg markiert ein weißes Andreaskreuz. Das Nahverkehrsnetz ist sehr gut ausgebaut; auch kürzere Teilstrecken sind deshalb leicht möglich.

The Ruhr hillside route is the best choice for visitors wishing to hike through scenic countryside in the Ruhr. Unlike the Ruhr Valley cycle path it hardly passes through the valley itself, but follows the contours of the wooded slopes. Castle ruins like Hohensyburg, Isenburg and Blankenstein afford spectacular views. The route alternates here between beech forest paths and comfortble farmedr roads. The suggested route can be covered in two to three days. The undulating countryside with a succession of steep climbs and descents requires a fair degree of fitness. The route is marked by a white diagonal cross (St. Andrew's cross). The good transport infrastructure enables you to follow shorter sections of the route.

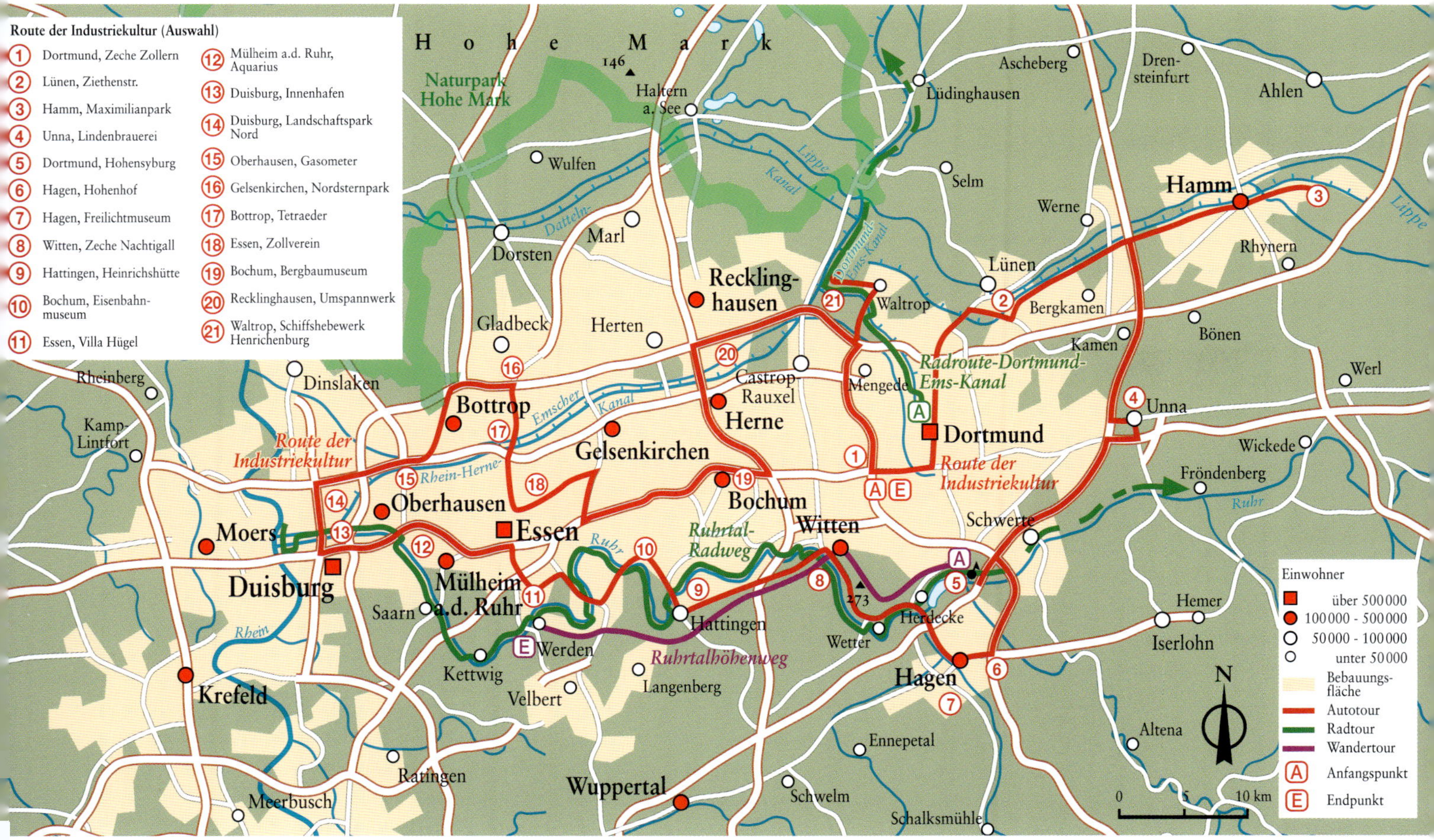

Ereignisse und Feste im Jahreskreis

Events and celebrations around the year

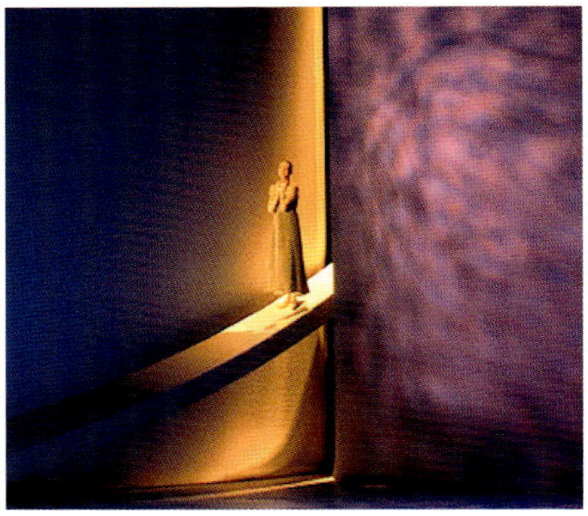

Frühling (Spring)

Internationales Frauenfilmfestival Dortmund/Köln (April)
Deutschlands wichtigste Frauenfilmfestival gastiert in jährlichem Wechsel in Dortmund oder Köln.
Germany's most important women's film festival alternates each year between Dortmund and Cologne.

Wittener Tage für Neue Kammermusik (Ende April/End of April)
Markenzeichen der Wittener Tage sind die ungewöhnlichen Veranstaltungsorte wie die Zeche Nachtigall, das Haus Witten oder das Märkische Museum.
The main feature of the Wittener Tage is the unusual choice of location, including the Nachtigall colliery, Haus Witten and the Märkisches Museum.

Duisburger Akzente (April, Mai/May)
Motto ist jedes Jahr ein anderes aktuelles Thema, dessen Facetten Veranstaltungen aus Theater, bildender Kunst, Literatur, Tanz und Wissenschaft beleuchten.
The theme each year is a topical subject which is then portrayed through events from the fields of drama, fine art, literature, dance and science.

Internationale Kurzfilmtage Oberhausen (Anfang Mai/Beginning of May)
Jedem Cineasten ein Begriff sind die Kurzfilmtage, die als ältestes Kurzfilmfestival der Welt gelten.
The Kurzfimtage (Oberhausen Short Film Festival) are known to cinema fans throughout the world, since it is considered to be the oldest of its kind in the world.

Ruhrfestspiele (1. Mai – Mitte Juni/1 May – Mid June))
Jedes Jahr am 1. Mai beginnen in Recklinghausen die Ruhrfestspiele, eines der ältesten Theaterfestivals Europas.
The Ruhr Festival starts every year in Recklinghausen on 1 May. It is one of the oldest drama festivals in Europe.

Mülheimer Theatertage (Mai – Juni/May – June)
Auf dem Forum für deutschsprachige Gegenwartsdramatik wird der Mülheimer Dramatikerpreis für das beste deutsche Bühnenstück vergeben.
The Mülheimer Dramatikerpreis (Mülheim Playwrights' Prize) is awarded to the best of the plays at the Forum for Contemporary German Drama.

moers festival (Pfingsten/Whitsun)
Beim „moers festival" kommen Jazzfans aus ganz Deutschland jedes Jahr zu Pfingsten voll auf ihre Kosten.
Every year at Whitsun jazz fans from all over Germany will find what they are looking for at the "moers festival".

Sommer (Summer)

Klavier-Festival Ruhr (Mai – Juli/May – July)
Das Klavier-Festival Ruhr hat sich unter dem Motto „das Ruhrgebiet beflügeln" rasch zu einer der wichtigsten Veranstaltungen ihrer Art entwickelt.
The Ruhr Piano Festival has rapidly grown into one of the most important events of its kind. Its motto is "Das Ruhrgebiet beflügeln" (Inspiring the Ruhr).

ExtraSchicht (Juni/June)
Überregional bekannt ist die „Nacht der Industriekultur", bei der außergewöhnliche Örtlichkeiten im Ruhrgebiet ihre Türen für unterschiedlichste kulturelle Veranstaltungen öffnen.
The "Nacht der Industriekultur" (Night of Industrial Culture) is famous beyond the regional boundaries; unusual locations open their doors to a wide range of cultural perfomances.

Sommerfestspiele Xanten (Juni – August/June – August)
Das römische Amphitheater im Archäologischen Park ist Mittelpunkt der Sommerfestspiele Xanten mit unterschiedlichen Aufführungen vor der Kulisse des historischen Theaters.
The Roman amphitheater in the Archeological Park provides the arena for various performanXanten's summer festival.

Zeltfestival Ruhr (August – September)
Für 17 Tage verwandelt sich das Ufer des Kemnader Sees in eine Zeltstadt mit Markt und viel Kultur.

For 17 days the shores of the Kemnader See are transformed into a tented town complete with market and lots of culture.

Bochum Total (Juli/July)

Beim größten kostenlosen Open-Air-Musikfestival Europas präsentieren mehr als 70 Bands ihr Können.

More than 70 bands demonstrate their skills at the biggest free open-air music festival in Europe.

Cranger Kirmes (August)

Eines der größten Volksfeste Deutschlands findet Anfang August im Herner Stadtviertel Crange statt.

One of the biggest local fairs in Germany takes place in August in the Crange district of Herne.

ComedyArts Festival Moers (August)

Freunde des guten Humors pilgern im August nach Moers. Bei Deutschlands ältestem Comedy Festival ist für jeden Geschmack etwas geboten.

Lovers of good humor head for Moers in August. Germany's oldest comedy festival can offer something for every taste.

RuhrTriennale (Juli–Oktober/July–October)

Auch die RuhrTriennale macht – wie die ExtraSchicht – aus Industriedenkmälern außergewöhnliche Veranstaltungsorte für Veranstaltungen in den Bereichen Musik, Schauspiel und Oper.

Like ExtraSchicht, the RuhrTriennale transforms industrial monuments into unusual settings for performances of music, drama and opera.

Essen Original (August)

Zehn Bühnen und über 1000 Mitwirkende verwandeln drei Tage lang die ganze Essener Innenstadt in ein einziges Open-Air Fest.

For three days, ten stages and a cast of over 1000 transform Essen city center into a vast open-air celebration.

KlassikSommer Hamm (August–September)

Im Zentrum des KlassikSommer Hamm steht die menschliche Stimme mit Liederabenden, Chormusik und Oper.

The main focus of the KlassikSommer Hamm is the human voice with evenings of lieder, choir music and opera.

Herbst (Fall)

Familien Drachenfest Lünen (Herbst)

Immer am ersten Wochenende der Herbstferien erobern bunte Flugdrachen den Himmel über Lünen.

Brightly-colored kites conquer the skies above Lünen on the first weekend of the fall half-term holidays.

Essener Lichtwochen (Oktober – Januar/October – January)

Ab Ende Oktober erstrahlt die Essener Innenstadt im Glanz einer Vielzahl großdimensionaler Lichtkunstwerke. Seit 2001 stehen die Lichtwochen im Zeichen der Europäischen Union, jedes Jahr ist das vielseitige Programm einem anderen EU-Mitgliedsstaat gewidmet.

From the end of October, Essen city center sparkles with numerous large-size light installations. Since 2001 the Lichtwochen have focused on the European Union; every year the wide-ranging program is devoted to a different member state of the EU.

Winter (Winter)

Weihnachtsmärkte

Zu den größten und bekanntesten Weihnachtsmärkten zählen die Märkte in Bochum, Dortmund, Duisburg, Oberhausen und Essen.

Among the largest and most famous Christmas markets are the markets in Bochum, Dortmund, Duisburg, Oberhausen and Essen.

Orgel PLUS, Bottrop (Januar/January)

Im Zentrum steht die Orgel kombiniert mit anderen Instrumenten.

The festival focuses on the organ combined with other instruments.

Up To Dance Festival, Gladbeck (Januar–Februar/ January–February)

Zwei Tage lang dreht sich in Gladbeck alles um den Tanz unterschiedlichster Stilrichtungen.

For two days everything in Gladbeck revolves around dance in a wide variety of forms.

Register | *Index*

Verweise auf Abbildungen sind kursiv | *References to pictures are in italics*

Moderne Skulptur aus Edelstahl im Gruga-Park, Essen.

Steel sculpture in the Gruga Park, Essen.

Bad Neuenahr

BAD NEUENAHR-AHRWEILER

SCHÖNING VERLAG

4 004545 115386

Neuenah 299

Fon (04 51) 31 03-0 · Fax (04 51) 3 10 31 30 · 001.53471.0299

4 004545 000019

Preisgruppencode

Deutschland ist schön – wir zeigen es!

Bibliografische Information Der Deutschen Nationalbibliothek
Die Deutsche Nationalbibliothek verzeichnet diese Publikation in der Deutschen Nationalbibliografie; detaillierte bibliografische Daten sind im Internet unter http://dnb.d-nb.de abrufbar.

Deutsche Originalausgabe

Ein Unternehmen der La Martinière Groupe

Alle Fotos Rainer Kiedrowski, Ratingen, mit Ausnahme von

S.49 o.re.: picture alliance/dpa (Alfried Krupp von Bohlen und Halbach);
S.66 u.li.: Ruhrfestspiele Recklinghausen/Torsten Janfeld.

Text und Konzeption: Dr. Reinhard Pietsch
Redaktion: Cornelia Schmidt
Touren: Bernhard Pollmann, Emden-Larrelt
Grundlayout: Christine Paxmann text • konzept • grafik
Satz: medienpartner.münchen
Kartographie: Heidi Schmalfuß, München
Lithografie: Repro-Ludwig, A-Zell am See
Druck und Bindung: Mohn Media, Gütersloh
Printed in Germany

ISBN 978-3-86873-110-1

www.knesebeck-verlag.de